DEVELOPMENT CENTRE STUDIES

THE BALANCE OF PAYMENTS EFFECTS OF EXTERNAL SHOCKS AND OF POLICY RESPONSES TO THESE SHOCKS

IN NON-OPEC DEVELOPING COUNTRIES

by

Bela Balassa
André Barsony
Anne Richards

DEVELOPMENT CENTRE
OF THE ORGANISATION FOR ECONOMIC CO-OPERATION AND DEVELOPMENT

The Organisation for Economic Co-operation and Development (OECD) was set up under a Convention signed in Paris on 14th December 1960, which provides that the OECD shall promote policies designed:

— to achieve the highest sustainable economic growth and employment and a rising standard of living in Member countries, while maintaining financial stability, and thus to contribute to the development of the world economy;
— to contribute to sound economic expansion in Member as well as non-member countries in the process of economic development;
— to contribute to the expansion of world trade on a multilateral, non-discriminatory basis in accordance with international obligations.

The Members of OECD are Australia, Austria, Belgium, Canada, Denmark, Finland, France, the Federal Republic of Germany, Greece, Iceland, Ireland, Italy, Japan, Luxembourg, the Netherlands, New Zealand, Norway, Portugal, Spain, Sweden, Switzerland, Turkey, the United Kingdom and the United States.

The Development Centre of the Organisation for Economic Co-operation and Development was established by decision of the OECD Council on 23rd October 1962.

The purpose of the Centre is to bring together the knowledge and experience available in Member countries of both economic development and the formulation and execution of general policies of economic aid; to adapt such knowledge and experience to the actual needs of countries or regions in the process of development and to put the results at the disposal of the countries by appropriate means.

The Centre has a special and autonomous position within the OECD which enables it to enjoy scientific independence in the execution of its task. Nevertheless, the Centre can draw upon the experience and knowledge available in the OECD in the development field.

Publié en français sous le titre :

LES EFFETS EXERCÉS
SUR LA BALANCE DES PAIEMENTS
PAR LES CHOCS EXTÉRIEURS
ET LES MESURES PRISES
POUR Y RÉPONDRE

DANS LES PAYS EN DÉVELOPPEMENT NON MEMBRES DE L'OPEP

***

CONTENTS

ANNEXES

LIST OF TABLES

Annexes

PREFACE

If co-operative action between North and South is to help alleviate present economic difficulties, it is important to understand as clearly as possible what has happened to the economies of the developing countries since 1973. For this purpose, OECD's Development Centre has undertaken an analysis of the 1973-78 experience of eight non-OPEC developing countries and one OECD Member country (Portugal) as well as seven groups of non-OPEC developing countries.

The predicament of the developing countries is commonly thought to be one of serious balance-of-payments deficits and high levels of debt. But this stereotype conceals considerable diversity, this study has found. First of all, they differ as regards the external shock suffered through the deterioration of their terms of trade and the slowdown of demand for their exports. Second, they differ in terms of the policy responses to these shocks.

Economists do not agree on which of the external shocks to the balance of payments of the developing countries have been the dominant ones. Some hold that the unfavourable effects of the 1974-75 world recession, the slowness of the subsequent recovery and the pressures for increased protection in the developed countries outweight in importance the adverse effects of the rise in the price of oil; others think the reverse is true. The Development Centre study analyses the impact of the various shocks in quantitative terms. The finding is that, for almost all the countries and the country groups concerned, the damage caused by deteriorating terms of trade – mainly due to the rise in the relative price of oil but also to that of manufactured imports – has been greater than the effects of the slowdown in developing countries' exports to the developed world. The export effect has become more important over the years but, except for two less industrialised country groups, has never assumed as much weight as the deterioration of the terms of trade. The importance of changes in terms of trade is especially marked in the case of the more industrialised developing countries. This suggests that, with industrialisation, developing countries become more vulnerable to changes in terms of trade and less vulnerable to changes in foreign demand for their exports as their economies become more energy intensive and the share of manufactured goods in total exports rises.

The results provide little evidence of damage to developing countries' exports due to increased protectionism in the developed countries. In fact, the income elasticity of demand in the developed nations for the manufactured exports of developing countries was higher during the 1973-78 period than in the preceding decade. This has offset in part the decline in developing countries' exports caused by lower economic growth rates in the developed world. Developing countries' exports also benefited from high economic growth in other developing countries where demand for imports of manufactured goods rose faster than income. Trade with the centrally-planned economies, on the other hand, provided no impetus to developing countries' exports, because growth slowed down in those countries and their demand for manufactured goods from developing nations fell more than income.

The policy responses of the countries and country groups to the external shocks also differed markedly. Some of the countries increased their borrowing abroad while others used domestic policy measures aimed at promoting exports, replacing imports, and slowing down the rate of economic growth. These policy responses, and their economic effects, are examined in considerable detail in the volume.

What are the implications of this experience for policy in the developing countries in response to the second round of oil price increases? They point up the importance of domestic policy measures, including the establishment of an appropriate system of incentives to increase exports and to substitute domestic for foreign goods, the maintenance of realistic exchange rates, and of positive real interest rates to encourage savings and investments as well as measures to enhance the efficiency of public investment. Application of such measures would also contribute to the efficient use of the proceeds of foreign borrowing.

This OECD Development Centre project consists of two phases. The first, a comparative analysis of economic policy measures adopted by the developing countries in response to external shocks after 1973, and of the economic effects of these measures, provides a clearer understanding of the adjustment process and serves as a reference for management of future shocks. The second phase will be a comparative study of changes in incentives and public investment decisions, analysing the long-term consequences of the adjustment policies adopted in response to external shocks.

The present volume presents the results of the first phase of the project. The analytical framework developed by Professor Bela Balassa from The Johns Hopkins University provided a common denominator for country as well as country group studies. Under co-operative arrangements with institutes in eight developing countries and one OECD Member country, the Centre's partners assumed intellectual and material responsibility for the studies of their respective countries. I wish to express my appreciation to the authors of the country studies and their institutions. They are as follows:

Brazil	Antonio Carlos Lemgruber	Centro de Estudos Monetários e de Economica International
	Roberto Fendt, Jr.	Fundaçao Centro de Estudos do Comércio Exterior
	Paulo Nogueira Batista, Jr.	Centro de Estudos Monetários e de Economica International
Colombia	Mauricio Carrizosa-Serrano	Fundacion para la Educacion Superior y el Desarrollo
Ivory Coast	Gaspard Kouadio Gbaka	Ministère de l'Economie des Finances et du Plan
	Michel Noël	The Johns Hopkins University
Malaysia	Yeoh Chian Imm Tan Tat Wai	Bank Negara
Mexico	Ernesto Zedillo	Banco de Mexico
Peru	Roberto Abusada Salah	Universidade Catolica
Portugal	Abel M. Mateus with the collaboration of Jaime P. Oliveira	Banco de Portugal
South Korea	Soogil Young	Korea International Economic Institute
Tunisia	Mohamed Rachid Kechiche	Institut d'Economie Quantitative "Ali Bach Hamba"

This project was a key part of the Development Centre research programme on INTERDEPENDENCE AND DEVELOPMENT, which was the major element of the Centre's research work over the three year period 1979-1981.

Bela Belassa, André Barsony and Anne Richards, directed the project, prepared this volume and are, in accordance with the norms existing at the Centre, responsible for its conclusions. The quality of their work greatly deserves the appreciation of the Centre.

Finally, I would like to express my special gratitude to the Government of Canada for the generous grant given by the Canadian International Development Agency (CIDA), which made possible the undertaking of the first phase of the project.

Professor Louis SABOURIN
President
OECD Development Centre

Chapter I

SUMMARY AND CONCLUSIONS

by Bela Balassa

1. ANALYSING EXTERNAL SHOCKS AND POLICY RESPONSES

Introduction

The non-OPEC developing countries suffered various external shocks after 1973. In the 1973-78 period, these shocks included the quadrupling of petroleum prices, which took full effect in 1974, and the world recession of 1974-75, which was followed by a relatively slow recovery. There were also pressures for increased protection in the developed countries during this period.

The quadrupling of petroleum prices adversely affected the balance of payments of most non-OPEC developing countries. Its effect was aggravated by the deterioration in the non-oil terms of trade in the case of some of the countries and alleviated by improvements in the non-oil terms of trade in the case of others. In several non-OPEC countries, in particular those exporting cocoa and coffee, a net improvement in the terms of trade ensued.

The slowdown in foreign demand for their exports, whether due to lower rates of economic growth or increased protection, also has adverse effects on the balance of payments of the non-OPEC developing countries, varying from country to country, depending on the composition of exports.

Countries where terms-of-trade and export volume effects combined gave rise to a deterioration in the balance of payments, adopted a variety of policy measures to alleviate these adverse consequences. Responses included increased reliance on external financing, export promotion and import substitution, and macroeconomic policy measures affecting exports and imports indirectly through a decrease in the rate of economic activity.

Needless to say, countries may also have followed a combination of policies, some of which had positive, and others negative, impacts on their balance of payments. Thus, a country suffering adverse external shocks may nevertheless have attempted to accelerate the rate of economic growth by relying on foreign borrowing and on import substitution to safeguard its balance-of-payments position.

Particular policy measures may also have been taken independently of external shocks, or may themselves have constituted an "internal shock". An excessively expansionary fiscal policy, financed by foreign borrowing, provides an example of such a shock. The economic effects of political change also come under this heading.

The present study sets out to examine the effects of external and internal shocks and of the policies applied in selected non-OPEC developing countries and country groups in the 1973-78 period. This Chapter briefly describes the analytical framework employed and summarizes the results for nine countries and for seven country groups. It also provides an evaluation of the results and draws implications for policy responses to the second oil shock.

External Shocks

The external shocks analysed in this study include changes in the terms of trade and the slowdown of foreign demand for the exports of the developing countries. The balance-of-payments effects of these shocks have been estimated by postulating a situation that would have existed in the absence of external shocks.

Terms of trade effects have been calculated as the difference between the current value of exports and imports and their constant price values, estimated in the prices of the 1971-73 ("1972") base period. They have further been decomposed into a "pure terms-of-trade effect", calculated on the assumption that the balance of trade expressed in terms of "1972" prices was in equilibrium, and an "unbalanced trade effect", indicating the impact of the rise of import prices on the deficit (surplus) in the balance of trade expressed in "1972" prices. This procedure reflects the assumption that price increases since "1972" have been due to external shocks, in particular, the direct and indirect effects of the quadrupling of oil prices.

In turn, the balance-of-payments effects of the slowdown in foreign demand on the exports of the developing countries have been calculated as the difference between the trend value of exports and hypothetical exports. The trend value of exports has been derived on the assumption that the growth rate of foreign demand for particular export products and product groups remained the same as in the 1963-73 period and that the country (country group) concerned maintained its "1972" share in these exports. In turn, hypothetical exports have been estimated on the assumption that the country maintained its "1972" market share in the actual exports of particular products and product groups. In the case of manufactured goods, the effects of changes in foreign GNP growth rates and of changes in foreign income elasticities of import demand (the ratio of the rate of growth of imports to that of GNP) have further been distinguished.

Policy Responses

This study considers policy responses to external shocks that involve additional net external financing, export promotion, import substitution, and the effects of macroeconomic policies on the rate of economic growth. The balance-of-payments effects of these policies have been estimated by postulating a situation that would have occurred in the absence of external shocks. However, the methodology applied does not separate the balance-of-payments effects of policy changes taken in response to external shocks from the effects of autonomous policy changes, that may themselves constitute an internal shock. Such distinction is necessarily a matter of interpretation.

Additional net external financing has been derived as the difference between the actual merchandise trade balance and the trade balance that would have obtained had trends in imports and exports (observed in the 1963-73 period) continued and import and export prices remained at their "1972" level. Trend values for non-factor services and private transfers do not enter into the calculation of additional net external financing as these flows are assumed to be unaffected by external shocks. However, in countries where tourism and workers' remittances are of importance, these have been treated in the same way as merchandise exports.

The effects of export promotion have been calculated as increases in exports above the country's "1972" export market shares. In turn, import substitution has been defined as savings in imports associated with a decrease in the income elasticity of import demand in the country in question.

Finally, the effects on imports of changes in GNP growth rates in response to the macroeconomic policies followed have been calculated on the assumption of unchanged income elasticities of import demand in the particular country. This relates to the impact of short-term policies, while long-term growth performance is affected by the allocation of existing and incremental resources and the rate of saving.

In the discussion of the cases of individual countries (country groups), the combined balance-of-payments effects of domestic policies which affect exports, import substitution, and GNP growth rates will also be noted. Additional net external financing, then, will equal the difference between the balance-of-payments effects of external shocks and the effects of domestic policies.

2. ESTIMATES FOR NINE NON-OPEC DEVELOPING COUNTRIES

Country Classification

The nine non-OPEC developing countries covered in this study divide into three groups, defined with respect to the character of external shocks and the existence of internal shocks. The first group includes Brazil, Korea and Tunisia, all of which suffered substantial adverse external shocks in the form of the deterioration in their terms of trade and the slowdown in foreign demand for their export products.

The second group of countries, comprising Mexico, Peru, and Portugal, also suffered considerable adverse external shocks and further experienced internal shocks. Internal shocks included expansionary fiscal policies in Mexico (the growth of Mexican oil exports affected the results only towards the end of the period under consideration), the April 1974 revolution in Portugal, and the military takeover in Peru.

External shocks were, on balance, favourable in the third group of countries, comprising Colombia, the Ivory Coast, and Malaysia, as improvements in their terms of trade more than offset the export shortfall due to the slowdown in foreign demand for their export products. The increase in the price of coffee benefited Colombia and the Ivory Coast, which also enjoyed the cocoa price rise. In turn, the increase in rubber and tin prices favoured Malaysia, that also had a growing export surplus in petroleum.

Estimates for each of the years 1974 to 1977, together with averages for the years 1974-75, 1976-77, and 1974-77 are shown in Tables III-1 to III-5 and Appendix Tables A-III-1 and A-III-2. A summary of the results is provided in Table I-1 while Table I-2 contains growth rates and macroeconomic data.

External Shocks

In the year 1974-75, the adverse terms of trade effects, due largely to the quadrupling of petroleum prices, much exceeded the export volume effects in the countries of the first two groups, the only exception being Tunisia which benefited from high phosphate prices. Terms-of-trade effects declined and export volume effects increased in subsequent years. Nevertheless, except for Mexico and Tunisia, where the expansion of petroleum exports led to improvements, terms-of-trade effects continued to exceed export volume effects by a substantial margin.

Among the countries of the third group, Malaysia was a net exporter of petroleum and benefited from increases in the prices of its principal traditional exports, rubber and tin. Colombia was also a net exporter of petroleum during much of the period under consideration and benefited from the rise in the price of coffee. Finally, increases in cocoa and coffee prices gave rise to a terms-of-trade gain in the Ivory Coast, despite its net import of petroleum.

The results show the importance of the rise in petroleum prices for the oil importing countries and conflict with the view that places emphasis on the unfavourable effects of the 1974-75 world recession and the subsequent slow recovery. These conclusions gain in force if we consider that the quadrupling of oil prices was an important factor contributing to the world recession, both directly and indirectly, by triggering the application of strong deflationary policies in the developed countries aimed at reducing the rate or inflation and safeguarding their balance-of-payments position.

Nor do the results provide evidence of the adverse effects of increased protectionism in the developed countries on the developing countries' exports of manufactured goods. In fact, the "ex post" income elasticity of import demand in the developed countries for the manufactured goods of the developing countries (defined as the ratio of the rate of growth of these imports to that of GNP in the developed countries) was higher during the period under consideration than in the preceding decade, offsetting in part the unfavourable effects of lower economic growth rates. While this elasticity measure result was also affected by supply factors in the developing countries, it nevertheless indicates the availability of markets in the developed countries for the manufactured exports of the developing countries.

In relation to intra-LDC trade, increases in income elasticities of import demand reinforced the beneficial effects of higher GNP growth rates. By contrast, centrally planned economies had lower growth rates *and* income elasticities of import demand for the manufactured goods of the developing countries.

Policy Responses

Group I

In 1974-75, on average, the combined balance-of-payments effects of external shocks amounted to 4 per cent of GNP in Brazil, 15 per cent in Korea, and 1 per cent in Tunisia. The corresponding figures for 1976-77 were 2 per cent in Brazil, 7 per cent in Korea, and 9 per cent in Tunisia.

In **Brazil**, the immediate response to external shocks was to increase foreign borrowing for the sake of maintaining high rates of economic growth. In the years 1974-75, the deterioration in the balance of payments resulting from external shocks was fully financed from abroad. Import substitution was practically nil as imports increased rapidly in 1974, while increases in export market shares substantially compensated for the rise in imports associated with higher GNP growth rates, as compared to the 1963-73 period.

Apart from permitting continued increases in domestic consumption, the amounts borrowed were employed to finance large investments in infrastructure and in high-cost, capital-intensive import substituting industries producing immediate goods. Import substitution was also promoted by the use of preferential credits and protective measures.

These policies led to considerable import substitution in 1976-77, while gains in exports, resulting from increases in market shares declined, offsetting the import savings associated with the deceleration in economic growth. As import substitution came to exceed the balance-of-payments effects of external shocks, additional foreign borrowing gave way to reserve accumulation.

The accumulation of reserves in 1976-77 should, however, be considered in the light of the increased burden of interest payments and dividends that necessitated increased borrowing. As a result, net debt service (interest payments and amortization less interest receipts), expressed as a proportion of exports, nearly doubled between 1973 and 1978 while, the net external debt (the gross external debt less net reserve holdings), expressed as a percentage of GNP, increased two-and-a-half times.

Moreover, import substitution proved increasingly costly, raising incremental capital-output ratios to a considerable extent. As the inflow of foreign capital was not used to increase investment shares, the rate of growth of GNP declined as a result, falling from 12.1 per cent in 1970-73 to 7.3 per cent in 1973-76 and to 5.3 per cent in 1976-78.

Korea, too, increased reliance on foreign capital in response to the external shocks it suffered in 1974 and 1975. However, foreign borrowing was largely used to raise the level of investment as the government provided investment incentives and encouraged savings through the re-establishment of positive real interest rates.

As a result, Korea rapidly expanded its production for export as well as for domestic markets, with increases in export shares and import substitution, taken together, fully offsetting the adverse balance-of-payments effects of external shocks in 1974-75. In turn, additional net external financing paid for the increased imports associated with higher GNP growth rates.

Export expansion assumed increased importance relative to import substitution in 1976-77 as incentives to exports were increased and import liberalisation measures were taken. In the same period, the two effects combined came to exceed the adverse balance-of-payments effects of external shocks four-and-a-half-time; this permitted the accumulation of $ 1.3 billions in reserves, although the acceleration of economic growth added to the import bill.

With rapid increases in exports, Korea's net debt service ratio was lower in 1978 than in 1973. Increases in the net external debt ratio were also much smaller in Korea than in Brazil, reflecting the slower increase of external debt and the acceleration of GNP growth. After remaining at 8.9 per cent in 1973-76, the average annual rate of growth of GNP was 10.1 per cent in 1976-79. This is because the increase in investment shares more than offset the small rise in incremental capital-output ratios that was restrained by the continuation of outward-looking policies.

After favourable external shocks in 1974, **Tunisia's** terms of trade deteriorated, aggravating the adverse effects of world market conditions on its exports. Additional net external financing increased further as the rise in export market shares was far outweighed by increases in imports that were associated with increases in import shares and higher GNP growth rates, as compared to the 1963-73 period.

Increases in incremental capital-output ratios, due largely to inefficient public investment, however, contributed to a decline in GNP growth rates from 10.3 per cent in 1970-73 to 8.5 per cent in 1973-76, and to 7.0 per cent in 1976-79, although still exceeding the 6.1 per cent growth rate in 1963-73. Finally, with rising additional net external financing, the ratio of the net external debt to GNP nearly doubled between 1973 and 1978, although rapid increases in exports limited the rise of the net debt service ratio.

Group II

In 1974-75, on the average, the combined balance-of-payments effects of external shocks amounted to 1 per cent of GNP in Mexico, 8 per cent in Peru, and 7 per cent in Portugal. These effects remained at 1 per cent of GNP in Mexico in 1976-77 but increased to 14 per cent in Peru and 12 per cent in Portugal.

In **Mexico**, additional net external financing exceeded the balance-of-payments effects of external shocks by a substantial margin throughout the period, as savings in imports associated with lower growth rates did not suffice to offset the deterioration in the balance of payments that resulted from decreases in export market shares and increases in import shares. Theses changes in trade shares, in turn, reflected the direct and indirect effects of expansionary fiscal policies followed under the Echeverria Administration, which financed social expenditures as well as often unproductive public investments. The internal shocks represented by these policies gave rise to rapid inflation and to a decline in Mexico's competitiveness which was not offset by a devaluation until September 1976.

The devaluation and the restrictive monetary policies, which followed under the Administration of Lopez Portillo in 1977, led to increases in export shares and to reductions in import shares, but these changes were not sufficient to undo the adverse effects of the policies followed in earlier years. And while, aided by the *deus ex machina* of petroleum exports, additional net external financing declined, the rising interest payments on foreign debt contracted in earlier years necessitated increased borrowing abroad. As a result, the net debt service came to exceed the value of merchandise exports in 1978 while the net external debt reached one-third of GNP.

As the policies applied affected exports and import substitution unfavourably and in several cases public investments exhibited low productivity, incremental capital-output ratios increased to a considerable extent in Mexico. In turn, the average annual rate of growth of GNP fell from 6.0 per cent in 1970-73 to 3.3 per cent in 1974-76 and did not reach earlier levels even after the improvements in 1976-79, when the growth rate averaged 5.8 per cent.

Internal shocks, represented by the policies of the military regime of General Velasco, reinforced the adverse effects of external shocks in **Peru**. While, aided by favourable changes in the terms of trade, the rate of growth of GNP remained relatively high until 1973, the increasing overvaluation of the exchange rate, the chaotic management of the state enterprises, the increased government budget deficit, and the fall in private investment (in response to political and economic uncertainty) created increasing economic difficulties.

The negative balance-of-payments impact of internal policies affecting exports, import substitution, and the rate of economic growth averaged 6 per cent of GNP in 1974-75 in Peru. With the adverse balance-of-payments effects of external shocks averaging 8 per cent, additional net external financing equalled 14 per cent of GNP during this period, necessitating substantial foreign borrowing that raised question concerning the country's creditworthiness.

Improved business confidence and the depreciation of the real exchange rate (the nominal exchange rate adjusted for changes in relative prices at home and abroad) under the government of General Bermudez led to a rise in export shares and to import in 1976 and 1977. However, increases in external shocks, together with interest payments on foreign debt contracted in earlier years, necessitated a further rise in foreign borrowing. After having reached one-half of the value of merchandise exports in 1975, the net debt service came to three-fourths of export value in 1978, when the net external debt surpassed one-half of GNP.

Peru's growing foreign indebtedness led to the adoption of deflationary policies in May 1978, resulting in a drop in GNP, averaging 1.7 per cent in 1976-79. The decline followed a fall in GNP growth rates from 5.6 per cent in 1970-73 to 3.6 per cent in 1974-76, as the rise in incremental capital-output ratios, due to the adverse effects of the policies followed, more than outweighed increases in investment shares.

In **Portugal**, the internal shock was the revolution of April 1974, which led to a substantial rise in government spending and to rapid increases in wages. In turn, profit rates declined as wage increases could not be compensated by price increases and disruptions in production reduced labour productivity. Exports to the developed countries fell as a result, reinforcing the adverse effects of the loss of markets in Portugal's former colonies which had become independant following the revolution.

Losses in export market shares continued in 1976 and 1977 and were not compensated by the fall in imports associated with the deceleration of economic growth and, to a lesser extent, import substitution. Following the Revolution there was a decline in GNP, averaging 0.9 per cent a year between 1973 and 1976, followed by a slow recovery, with a GNP growth rate of 3.8 per cent in 1976-79 compared to 8.6 per cent in 1970-73.

Portugal drew on its substantial gold holdings and borrowed abroad to finance the balance-of-payment deficit resulting from the adverse effects of external and internal shocks. Nevertheless, the net external debt ratio and the net debt service ratio remained at relatively low levels, hardly exceeding 20 per cent.

Groupe III

In **Colombia**, the adverse balance-of-payments effects of external shocks, averaging 1 per cent of GNP in 1974-75, gave place to favourable external shocks, amounting to 2 per cent of GNP in 1976-77. A similar pattern is shown in the Ivory Coast and in Malaysia. In both countries, the adverse balance-of-payments effects of external shocks, equivalent to 1 per cent of GNP in 1974-75, were followed by favourable external shocks, averaging 9 per cent of GNP in 1976-77.

The opportunity provided by improvements in the balance of payments was not utilised to accelerate the rate of growth of investment and of GNP in **Colombia**. Thus, notwithstanding increases from 5.6 per cent in 1973-76 to 6.6 per cent in 1976-79, the average annual rate of growth of GNP remained below the 7.0 per cent growth rate observed in 1970-73.

Changes in the system of incentives adversely affected exports and the domestic production of import substitutes. Export shares declined due to the combined effects of the appreciation of the real exchange rate and reductions in export subsidies, while import shares increased as a result of the joint impact of exchange rate changes and modest measures of import liberalisation.

With the adverse effects of domestic policies nearly offset by the favourable impact of external shocks on the balance of payments in 1974-77, on average, foreign borrowing declined in Colombia. Correspondingly, both the net external debt ratio and the net debt service ratio fell over time.

Notwithstanding the appreciation of irs real exchange rate, the **Ivory Coast** experienced increases in export market shares as a result of measures taken to encourage the expansion and diversification of primary and manufactured exports. But the appreciation of the real exchange rate contributed to increases in import shares which were aggravated by the high import intensity of rising investment in the second half of the period.

The effect of resulting increase in imports was, however, considerably smaller than that of the increase in export market shares, so that the combined effects of domestic policy measures on the balance of payments reinforced the impact of favourable external shocks in the Ivory Coast. Increases in foreign borrowing were nevertheless necessary, given the interest payments and dividends on foreign debt contracted, and foreign direct investment undertaken, in the previous period.

The proceeds of foreign borrowing were in part used in public investment projects which were often inefficient, raising incremental capital-output ratios. Nevertheless, with the rising share of investment, the average annual rate of growth of GNP reached 8.0 per cent in 1976-79, after having declined from 6.6 per cent in 1970-73 to 5.8 per cent in 1973-76. In turn, the net debt service ratio and the ratio of the net external debt to GNP approximately doubled between 1973 and 1978.

The depreciation of the real exchange rate led to increases in export market shares and import substitution in **Malaysia**, with promotional measures also favouring exports. The resulting increases in domestic production and profits, together with positive real interest rates, contributed to a rise in savings and investment in Malaysia. The effects of higher investment shares were however offset by increases in incremental capital-output ratios that may be explained by the difficulties experienced in connection with asset transfers to Malay nationals. Correspondingly, the rate of growth of GNP declined from 8.6 per cent in 1970-73 to 7.2 per cent in 1976-79. Nevertheless, growth rates were higher than in the 1963-73 period (6.4 per cent) and showed increases between 1973-76 (6.2 per cent) and 1976-79 (7.2 per cent).

With the positive balance-of-payments effects of domestic economic policies reinforcing the impact of favourable external shocks, Malaysia was able to accumulate reserves. While there was some foreign borrowing as a counterpart to interest payments on debt contracted in earlier years and dividend on foreign direct investment, the net debt service ratio and the ratio of the net external debt to GNP remained practically nil.

3. ESTIMATES FOR GROUPS OF NON-OPEC DEVELOPING COUNTRIES

The Classification Scheme

For purposes of this study, non-OPEC developing countries have been classified into six groups, depending on the level of industrialisation and the character of their principal exports. The six groups include:

1. The newly-industrialising developing countries.
2. Relatively industrialised developing countries, with economies based predominantly on agriculture.
3. Relatively industrialised developing countries, with economies based predominantly on mineral production.
4. Less industrialised developing countries, with economies based predominantly on agriculture.
5. Less industrialised developing countries, with economies based predominantly on mineral production.

and 6. Least developed countries[1].

1. The criteria used in the classification are described in Annex B.

Given their large size within the individual country groups, the 1971-72 war and subsequent drought, and the impossibility of separating data for Pakistan and Bangladesh for the 1963-73 period three countries of South Asia, India, Pakistan and Bangladesh, have been included in a seventh group.

Estimates for each of the years 1974 to 1978, together with averages for the years 1974-75, 1976-77, 1974-77, and 1974-78 are shown in Table IV-1 and IV-2 and Appendix Tables A-IV-1 and A-IV-2[1]. A summary of the results is provided in Table I-1, while Table I-2 contains growth rates and macroeconomic data.

External Shocks

The results obtained for the country groups confirm the conclusions reached in regard to individual developing countries subject to external shocks as far as the relative importance of terms of trade effects is concerned. In the years 1974-75, the adverse terms of trade effects, due largely to the quadrupling of petroleum prices, exceeded the adverse export volume effects by a considerable margin in all the country groups. The ratio of the two effects ranged from 9.1 in the newly-industrialising countries to 2.5 in the less industrialised agriculture-based economies.

With the slowdown in the rise of the price of petroleum in 1976-77, terms of trade losses declined in all the country groups, except for the relatively industrialised agriculture and mineral-based economies, with a reversal occuring in 1978. Less industrialised agriculture-based economies even experienced a terms of trade gain in 1976-77, as did the least developed countries in 1977, due largely to increases in coffee and cocoa prices, that gave place to a loss in 1978. In turn, all country groups experienced increases in the adverse export volume effects over time.

As a result of these changes, the ratio of terms-of-trade effects to export volume effects declined between 1974-75 and 1976-77 in each of the groups. The decline in the ratio was the largest in the three groups of countries at lower levels of industrial development, which enjoyed favourable price trends in their primary exports but suffered the adverse effects of the slow growth of world demand for these commodities. Changes in the ratio were smaller in the three groupes of more industrialised countries, which benefited from the relatively rapid growth of foreign demand for manufactured exports but were unfavourably affected by the deterioration in the terms of trade for manufactured goods. The latter consideration also apply to the countries of South Asia, where manufactured goods account for a relatively large proportion of exports.

In 1978, the ratio of terms of trade effects to export volume effects declined further in the more industrialised country groups, while a change in the opposite direction occurred in the less industrialised country groups, which suffered the consequences of declines in primary product prices. Nevertheless, for the 1974-78 period, taken as a whole, the ratio of terms-of-trade effects to export volume effects was larger in the more industrialised, than in the less industrialised, country groups.

Policy Responses

Group I

In the newly industrialising countries, the balance-of-payments effects of external shocks averaged 7 per cent of GNP in 1974-75 and declined to 6 per cent in subsequent years. While initially, the newly-industrialising countries met external shocks largely through foreign borrowing, the ratio of additional net external financing to the balance-of-payments effects of external shocks fell to 18 per cent in 1976-77 and turned negative in 1978, indicating a curtailed reliance on additional foreign capital. These changes reflected savings in imports due to import substitution and lower GNP growth rates, with export market effects being relatively small[2].

GNP growth rates declined from 8.3 per cent in 1970-73 to 4.7 per cent in 1973-79, notwithstanding a small increase in investment shares, indicating a near-doubling of incremental capital-output ratios. Among the newly industrialising countries studied, this ratio increased greatly in Brazil which promoted high-cost import substitution, in Mexico which followed excessively expansionary policies, and in Portugal, where the April 1974

1. Data for 1978 were not available for the less industrialised mineral-based group.

2. Note, however, that the newly industrialising countries accounted for much of the manufactured exports of the developing countries in the 1963-73 period, and hence could not appreciably increase their market shares subsequently. Had changes in market shares in manufactured goods been measured vis-à-vis developed country exporters, positive export market effects would have been shown for the group. See page 128 for further discussion.

Revolution represented an "internal shock" to the economy. By contrast, incremental capital-output ratios increased little and high economic growth rates were maintained in Korea, which continued to follow outward-oriented policies.

Korea also avoided the large increases in debt service and external debt ratios that occurred in the other three countries. Due to interest payments and amortization on debt contracted following the quadrupling of oil prices, the total financing requirements of the newly-industrialising countries continued to rise, partially offsetting favourable changes in additional net external financing.

Group II

In relatively industrialised developing countries, with economies based predominantly on agriculture, the balance-of-payments effects of external shocks averaged 5 per cent of GNP in 1974-75. The ratio rose to 6 per cent in 1976-77 and to 8 per cent in 1978, reflecting the deterioration in the terms of trade as well as adverse export volume effects. Additional net external financing exceeded the balance-of-payments effects of external shocks throughout the period, largely because of increases in import shares. This group of countries also experienced a slight loss in export market shares and small increases in imports due to higher GNP growth rates, as compared to the 1963-73 period.

GNP growth rates declined, however, towards the end of the period under consideration, averaging 6.6 per cent in 1973-79 as against 6.8 per cent in 1970-73. With investment shares rising by more than one-fourth, the result indicates increases in incremental capital-output ratios. Among individual countries, this was the case in Colombia as well as in Malaysia, reflecting the adverse effects of domestic policies in the first case and the difficulties encountered in asset transfers to Malay nationals in the second.

Colombia and Malaysia, discussed above, are not representative of the group of relatively industrialised agricultural countries, as they both experienced favourable external shocks, while the groupe as a whole suffered large adverse shocks. One may surmise that the domestic policies followed by the other countries of the group not only contributed to the deterioration of the balance of payments, but also led to increases in incremental capital-output ratios. At the same time, the increased burden of interest payments and amortization led to a near-doubling of total financing requirements for the group as a whole.

Group III

The third group of relatively industrialised developing countries with economies based predominantly on mineral production, suffered external shocks, the balance-of-payments effects of which average 4 per cent of GNP in1974-75. The ratio rose to 7 per cent in 1976-77 and to 9 per cent in 1978, as the prices of minerals, in particular, copper and phosphates, declined. The group covered three-fourths of the balance-of-payments effects of external shocks by additional net external financing throughout the period under consideration. Increases in export shares provided the remainder, while import savings due to lower GNP growth rates were offset by increases in import shares.

Among the countries of the group studied individually, additional net external financing exceeded the balance-of-payments effects of external shocks in Peru and Tunisia, implying that the only remaining large country - Chile - relied on domestic policy measures to offset the effects of external shocks. The results observed in Chile also largely explain why, after having declined from 3.9 per cent in 1970-73 to 1.6 per cent in 1973-76, the average GNP growth rate of the group rose to 4.0 per cent in 1976-79, since Peru and Tunisia experienced a continued decline in their rate of economic growth.

After having increased temporarily, the average share of investment in GDP in the group of relatively industrialised mineral-based countries returned to its 1970-73 level, indicating that the incremental capital-output ratio, too, regained its earlier level. With continued increases in the ratio in Peru and Tunisia, this result appears to have been due to favourable developments in Chile, which adopted outward-oriented policies during the period under consideration. Finally, available data indicate that Chile was largely responsible for the observed pattern of total external financing in this group, which reached a peak of 10 per cent of GNP in 1975, and fell to 7 per cent of GNP in 1977, as external financing needs declined.

Group IV

The group of less industrialised developing countries, with economies based primarily on agriculture, experienced external shocks, the balance-of-payments effects of which averaged 6 per cent of GNP in 1974-75. In turn, favourable external shocks (−1 per cent of GNP) were observed in 1976-77 when cocoa and coffee prices were high, giving place to unfavourable shocks (4 per cent of GNP) in 1978 when prices declined again.

The only country of the group studied individually, the Ivory Coast, experienced favourable external shocks due to high cocoa and coffee prices for the period as a whole. The Ivory Coast was also able to accumulate reserves as export shares increases in response to the relatively outward-oriented policies applied. It follows that the performance of the remainder of the group was even less favourable than the average result for the entire group, which had additional net external financing approximately double the balance-of-payments effects of external shocks, as losses in export market shares and increases in import shares each averaged one-half of the balance-of-payments effects of these shocks.

The ratio of total external financing to GNP did not, however, fully regain its 1975 level of 9 per cent, as GNP growth accelerated after 1976, reflecting an increase in the GNP of Ghana, the largest country of the group, after a substantial decline in 1973-76. As a result, average GNP growth rates for the group in the 1973-79 period equalled the 3.3 per cent growth rate for 1970-73. In the meantime, however, the share of investment in GDP increased by one-tenth.

Group V

Like the relatively industrialised mineral-producting countries, this group experienced increases in the balance-of-payments effects of external shocks from 5 per cent in 1974-75 to 7 per cent in 1976-77, as mineral prices declined. Data for the year 1978 are not available, and none of the countries of the group was studied individually.

From available evidence, it appears, however, that this group of countries was unable to utilise external financing to cushion the balance-of-payments effects of external shocks, as they were already heavily indebted in the preceding period. At the same time, lenders demanded the imposition of restrictive policies,which contributed to the stagnation of their economies following a GNP growth rate of 4.4 per cent in 1970-73.

Another factor contributing to their stagnation was the loss of export market shares which raised the adverse balance-of-payments effects of external shocks by over one-half. In turn, import savings due to increases in import shares, associated with the extreme scarcity of foreign exchange and economic stagnation, exceeded the balance-of-payments effects of external shocks by one-half.

With high interest payments and amortization on debt contracted in earlier years, total external financing in this group of less industrialised mineral-producing countries reached a high of 18 per cent of GNP in 1975. It subsequently declined to 16 per cent in 1976 and, again, to 9 per cent in 1977, as foreign borrowing and interest payments fell.

Group VI

The balance-of-payments effects of external shocks averaged 6 per cent of the GNP of the least developed countries in 1974-75. This ratio fell to 2 per cent in 1976-77, as coffee and cotton prices rose, but increased to 9 per cent in 1978, when the prices of these commodities fell again. None of the countries of the group was studied individually.

Additional net external financing exceeded the balance-of-payments effects of external shocks throughout the period under consideration. Losses in export market shares reached two-thirds of the balance-of-payments effects of external shocks and were not fully offset by import savings due to import substitution and a decline in GNP growth rates.

Apart from the previous country group, the least developed countries had the poorest growth record, with the GNP growth rate declining from 3.2 per cent in 1970-73 to 2.4 per cent in 1973-76 and to 1.7 per cent in 1976-79. This decline occurred despite increases in investment shares, reflecting a doubling of incremental capital-output ratios.

As in the case of the previous country group, poor export performance contributed to the decline of GNP growth rates in the least developed countries. At the same time, in contrast to the previous group, the balance-of-payments deficit of the least developed countries was financed in large part by foreign aid. Correspondingly, interest payments and amortisation remained low, although total external financing surpassed 10 per cent of GNP by the end of the period.

Group VII

The countries of South Asia were not studied individually. The balance-of-payments effects of external shocks averaged 3 per cent of the GNP of this group of countries, in 1974-75, declining to 2 per cent in 1976-77 and increasing again to 3 per cent in 1978. Additional net external financing exceeded the balance-of-payments effects of external shocks by nearly three-fourths in the 1974-78 period, on average, reflecting substantial increases in import shares and some losses in export market shares.

Rates of economic growth nevertheless increased from the depressed level of 1.3 per cent in 1970-73, when war and drought adversely affected the economies of the countries concerned. GNP growth rates averaged 4.6 per cent in 1973-79, with the share of investment in GDP exceeding its 1971-73 level by one-tenth. As the inflow of foreign aid and workers' remittances from the Middle East largely provided for the balance-of-payments needs of the countries of South Asia, foreign borrowing and total external financing remained low throughout the period.

4. POLICY IMPLICATIONS OF THE RESULTS

The results obtained for each of the country groups represent averages for countries which often had different experiences with external shocks and followed different policies. Accordingly, the following discussion will focus on the policy experience of the nine countries studies individually. It will be supplemented by evidence provided by estimates for the seven country groups, whenever appropriate.

The findings of the nine country studies point to the importance of incentive policies in responding to external shocks. The continuation of an outward-oriented development strategy, providing similar incentives to production destined for domestic and for foreign markets, led to rapid export expansion and efficient import substitution in Korea. Export incentives also contributed to increases in export market shares in the Ivory Coast, Malaysia, and Tunisa, while the opposite result obtained in Colombia, Mexico, and Portugal, where the overvaluation of the exchange rate and/or reductions in export subsidies adversely affected exports.

The data further indicate the existence of a positive correlation between increases in export shares and the rate of growth of GNP. Thus, the highest GNP growth rates were observed in Korea, Tunisia, the Ivory Coast, and Malaysia, where the ratio of export expansion, associated with increases in export market shares, to the gross national product exceeded 2 per cent. In turn, countries with losses in export market shares, including Colombia, Mexico, and Portugal, had relatively low rates of economic growth, while Brazil occupied a middle position in terms of exports as well as economic growth. Among the nine countries, only Peru does not fit the pattern as it gained export market shares but had the lowest GNP growth rate, due to the internal shocks it experienced.

The results point to the beneficial effects of outward orientation on economic growth. These effects appear to have operated through improvements in efficiency in the use of existing and incremental resources, as countries with favourable export performance also had the lowest incremental capital-output ratios. Economic growth further benefited from increases in investment shares that were the most pronounced in Korea, Tunisia and the Ivory Coast, where positive real interest rates and/or investment incentives favoured domestic savings and investment.

The relationship between reliance on external financing in response to external shocks and the rate of economic growth is of further interest. Among the nine countries under study, GNP growth rates were the lowest in Mexico, Peru, and Portugal, where additional net external financing exceeded the adverse balance-of-payments effects of external shocks during the period under consideration. In all three countries, internal shocks in the form of inappropriate policies contributed to this outcome.

Furthermore, GNP growth rates declined in Brazil, where one-half of the balance-of-payments effects of external shocks was met by additional net external financing, while Korea had the highest GNP growth rate as well as substantial reserve accumulation. However, in Tunisia, high rates of economic growth were associated with additional net external financing in excess of the adverse balance-of-payments effects of external shocks.

The observed differences may be explained by reference to the fact that the effects of external financing on economic growth depend on the uses to which the proceeds of foreign borrowing are put. In Tunisia and, in the early part of the period when it borrowed abroad, in Korea, the proceeds of foreign borrowing were used to raise the level of investment, with some increases in incremental capital-output ratios. By contrast, in Brazil, Mexico, Peru, and Portugal the proceeds were in large part used for increasing consumption and/or in high-cost investment activities that raised incremental capital-output ratios to a considerable extent. At the same time, foreign borrowing gave rise to high debt service charges and foreign indebtedness in the four countries.

Estimates for the seven groups of developing countries tend to support the findings of the country studies on the favourable effects of outward orientation for economic growth. Thus, excepting the relatively industrialised mineral-producing countries, incremental capital-output ratios were the highest, and GNP rates the lowest, in the three groups of less industrialised countries, which experienced large losses in export market shares during the period under consideration. In turn, the relatively industrialised agricultural countries gained market shares and showed the best growth performance, followed by the newly-industrialising countries and the countries of South Asia, which had small losses in export market shares.

While the relatively industrialised mineral-producing countries experienced favourable export performance with initially low GNP growth rates, economic growth accelerated after the effects of the Chilean reforms became apparent. The acceleration of growth was accomplished with the lowest investment shares among the seven groups. This contrasts with the less industrialised mineral-producing countries, which experienced economic stagnation, although they exhibited the highest investment shares.

There is no evidence of a correlation between the extent of additional net external financing in response to external shocks and the rate of economic growth among the seven groups of developing countries. At the same time, the results indicate the existence of considerable differences among them as regards reliance on external financing and on domestic policy measures in response to external shocks.

Whereas the use of domestic policy measures permitted the newly industrialising countries to reduce, and ultimately to eliminate, reliance on additional net external financing, such financing continued to exceed the balance-of- payments effects of external shocks in agriculture-based economies, including those of South Asia. The countries in question relied on foreign capital to avoid or to minimise the decline in the rate of economic growth and, with the exception of the least developed countries, used much of the inflow to increase the rate of investment. Finally, among mineral-based economies, about four-fifths of the balance-of-payments effects of external shocks were met by additional net external financing in the relatively industrialised countries, while in the less industrialised countries, their inability to obtain sufficient external financing necessitated the use of restrictive policies, which resulted in stagnation.

At the same time, debt service ratios and foreign indebtedness rose to a considerable extent in countries and country groups, which relied on additional net external financing to cushion the impact of external shocks on their economies. Apart from postponing domestic adjustment, then, reliance on external financing may create balance-of-payments problems in the future unless the loans are self-liquidating, in the sense that they generate foreign exchange earnings and/or savings, sufficient to repay the loan with interest.

These considerations are of particular relevance to developing countries experiencing the second oil shock. At the same time, several of these countries may encounter borrowing limitations, due to liquidity problems, even if the proceeds are used in investments that are self-liquidating in the long run. High interest rates further aggravate the liquidity problems and increase the cost of investing borrowed funds.

Given the existing indebtedness of the developing countries and the expectation that the real price of petroleum may increase or, at least, will not decline in the future, the need for domestic policies of adjustment will be readily apparent. To the extent possible, these policies should aim at increasing output rather than reducing expenditure. This purpose would be served by appropriate production incentives, including the maintenance of realistic exchange rates and the elimination of the bias against exports, as well as by incentives to save and to invest through positive real interest rates and the promotion of private investment.

TABLE I-1

REPRESENTATIVE RATIOS OF BALANCE OF PAYMENTS EFFECTS OF EXTERNAL SHOCKS

AND POLICY RESPONSES TO THESE SCHOCKS(a)

IN NINE NON-OPEC DEVELOPING COUNTRIES

	External shocks as a percentage of GNP			Terms of trade effects	Export volume effects	Additional net external financing	Increases in export market shares	Import sub-stitution	Effects of lower GNP growth rates	Net external debt ratio		Net debt service ratio	
	1974-75	1976-77	1974-77	as a percentage of external shocks, 1974-77 average						1973	1978	1973	1978
										percent			
Brazil	3.7	2.1	2.8	85	15	50	15	51	-16	36.4	61.4	6.8	17.6
Korea	14.5	6.5	10.1	76	24	-67	94	129	-56	13.1	11.9	13.9	19.2
Tunisia	0.9	9.0	5.5	35	65	206	40	-112	-34	23.6	27.5	21.4	36.1
Mexico	1.3	1.1	1.2	41	59	285	-101	-106	22	62.4	109.3	13.3	33.3
Peru	8.4	14.3	11.4	80	20	108	15	-20	-3	41.7	74.3	28.0	57.8
Portugal	6.9	12.0	9.5	59	41	112	-80	13	55	3.7	22.8	-13.4	21.8
Colombia	1.4	-2.0	-0.4	329	-229	-95	-61	-125	-9	26.5	13.4	13.0	3.7
Ivory Coast	1.5	-8.9	-4.2	223	-123	-275	229	-94	40	7.9	14.2	15.0	34.6
Malaysia	0.6	-8.7	-4.2	185	-85	-125	108	85	-168	-0.4	1.4	-7.1	-3.0

Note: (a) The signs are reversed in the case of Colombia, the Ivory Coast, and Malaysia, which experienced favourable external shocks.

TABLE I-2

DOMESTIC EXPENDITURE SHARES, INCREMENTAL CAPITAL-OUTPUT RATIOS AND GROWTH RATES IN NINE NON-OPEC DEVELOPING COUNTRIES

	1963-73	1970-73	1973-76	1976-79	1973-79	1963-73	1970-73	1973-76	1976-79	1973-79	1963-73	1970-73	1973-76	1976-79	1973-79
	BRAZIL					KOREA					TUNISIA				
DOMESTIC EXPENDITURE SHARES (as a percent of GDP, in current prices)															
Private Consumption	72.1	68.7	70.0	69.4	69.7	76.1	71.1	68.0	61.7	64.9	66.9	66.1	61.9	66.1	64.0
Public Consumption	10.7	9.7	9.7	9.6	9.6	10.3	10.3	10.6	11.3	10.9	16.1	15.0	13.8	16.2	15.0
Total Concumption	82.8	78.5	79.7	78.9	79.3	86.4	81.4	78.6	73.0	75.8	83.0	81.1	75.7	82.3	79.0
Gross Domestic Fixed Investment	18.2	22.9	24.4	22.4	23.4	21.4	22.3	24.8	29.2	27.0	22.4	20.0	25.3	28.7	27.0
Increases in Stocks	n.a.	n.a.	n.a.	n.a.	n.a.	1.8	1.8	3.5	1.9	2.7	0.7	0.8	3.1	0.2	1.6
Gross Domestic Investment	18.2	22.9	24.4	22.4	23.4	23.2	24.1	28.3	31.1	29.7	23.1	20.8	28.4	28.9	28.6
Net Foreign Investment	-1.0	-1.4	-4.0	-1.3	-2.7	-9.6	-5.5	-6.9	-4.1	-5.5	-6.1	-1.9	-4.1	-11.2	-7.6
INCREMENTAL CAPITAL-OUTPUT RATIOS	2.3	1.7	3.1	4.3	3.6	2.1	2.4	2.7	3.1	2.3	3.4	2.2	2.5	3.8	3.1
GROWTH RATES (constant prices)															
Gross National Product	8.0	12.1	7.3	5.3	6.2	9.1	8.9	8.9	10.1	10.1	6.1	10.3	8.5	7.0	7.4
Population	2.9	2.8	2.8	2.8	2.8	2.2	2.0	1.9	1.8	1.9	2.0	1.7	2.1	2.5	2.3
Per Capita GNP	5.2	9.2	4.5	2.4	3.4	6.9	6.8	7.0	8.3	8.3	4.2	8.6	6.5	4.5	5.1
	MEXICO					PERU					PORTUGAL				
DOMESTIC EXPENDITURE SHARES (as a percent of GDP, in current prices)															
Private Consumption	73.0	72.9	66.7	64.8	65.9	71.4	72.0	75.2	69.7	72.4	71.4	68.8	78.5	74.8	77.0
Public Consumption	7.9	8.6	10.9	11.6	11.2	11.8	12.7	13.0	12.4	12.7	13.3	13.6	14.7	14.3	14.5
Total Consumption	80.9	81.5	77.6	76.4	77.1	83.2	84.7	88.2	82.1	85.1	84.7	82.4	93.2	89.1	91.5
Gross Domestic Fixed Investment	20.1	19.2	21.8	21.3	21.6	14.0	12.7	16.4	14.3	15.4	18.6	19.9	19.5	20.1	19.7
Increases in Stocks	n.a.	0.4	3.0	2.7	2.9	2.2	2.3	2.3	0.4	1.3	2.0	4.2	1.2	4.1	2.4
Gross Domestic Investment	20.1	19.6	24.9	24.0	24.5	16.2	15.0	18.7	14.7	16.7	20.6	24.1	20.7	24.2	22.1
Net Foreign Investment	-1.0	-1.1	-2.5	-0.4	-1.6	0.6	0.3	-6.9	3.2	-1.8	-5.3	-6.5	-13.9	-13.3	-13.6
INCREMENTAL CAPITAL-OUTPUT RATIOS	3.1	3.0	3.8	5.5	4.1	3.1	3.5	3.9	-5.5	5.9	2.9	2.3	14.5	6.3	4.0
GROWTH RATES (constant prices)															
Gross National Product	6.4	6.0	3.3	5.8	4.2	4.9	5.6	3.6	-1.7	0.4	7.4	8.6	-0.9	3.8	2.0
Population	3.2	3.2	3.3	3.3	3.3	2.8	2.7	2.7	2.8	2.8	-0.2	1.9	1.7	1.1	1.4
Per Capita GNP	3.2	2.7	0.0	2.5	0.9	2.1	2.8	0.9	-4.4	-2.4	7.6	6.6	-2.6	2.7	0.6
	COLOMBIA					IVORY COAST					MALAYSIA				
DOMESTIC EXPENDITURE SHARES (as a percent of GDP, in current prices)															
Private Consumption	74.0	72.9	72.1	67.1	69.1	61.4	62.6	58.4	54.1	56.7	62.1	59.2	55.6	51.8	53.7
Public Consumption	7.3	8.2	7.2	7.1	7.2	14.9	15.7	16.2	14.7	15.6	16.7	17.3	16.1	15.8	16.0
Total Consumption	81.3	81.1	79.3	74.2	76.8	76.3	77.3	74.6	68.8	72.3	78.8	76.5	71.7	67.6	69.7
Gross Comestic Fixed Investment	18.2	18.9	18.8	20.0	19.4	18.5	20.8	21.2	28.2	24.0	17.9	21.6	24.6	24.6	24.6
Increases in Stocks	1.6	1.0	1.4	3.5	2.4	1.3	1.0	1.3	0.9	1.1	n.a.	n.a.	n.a.	n.a.	n.a.
Gross Domestic Investment	19.8	20.0	20.2	23.5	21.8	19.8	21.8	22.5	29.1	25.1	17.9	21.6	24.6	24.6	24.6
Net Foreign Investment	1.1	1.1	0.5	2.3	1.4	3.9	0.9	2.9	2.1	2.6	3.3	1.9	3.7	7.8	5.7
INCREMENTAL CAPITAL-OUTPUT RATIOS	3.6	2.8	3.8	2.9	3.2	2.5	2.6	2.2	3.7	3.0	2.5	2.1	3.4	2.9	3.1
GROWTH RATES (constant prices)															
Gross National Product	5.6	7.0	4.6	6.6	5.5	6.5	6.6	5.8	8.0	7.3	6.4	8.6	6.2	7.2	6.9
Population	2.7	2.3	2.3	2.2	2.3	4.2	6.1	5.7	4.3	5.0	2.9	2.8	2.7	2.6	2.6
Per Capita GNP	2.9	4.7	2.3	4.4	3.2	2.3	0.6	0.1	3.6	2.3	3.5	5.9	3.5	4.6	4.3

Source: World Bank data base

Note: Data for Expenditure Shares do not include initial year in each period.

TABLE I-3

REPRESENTATIVE RATIOS OF BALANCE OF PAYMENT EFFECTS OF EXTERNAL SHOCKS AND POLICY RESPONSES TO THESE SHOCKS

IN SEVEN NON-OPEC DEVELOPING COUNTRY GROUPS

	External shocks as a percentage of GNP				Ratio of terms of trade effects to export volume effects				Terms of trade effects	Export volume effects	Additional net external financing	Increases in export market shares	Import substitution	Effects of lower GNP growth rates
	1974-75	1976-77	1978	1974-78	1974-75	1976-77	1978	1974-78	As a percentage of external shocks(a)					
Newly Industrialising Countries	7.0	5.6	6.1	6.2	9.1	3.9	2.2	4.5	82	18	39	-1	35	27
Relatively Industrialised Countries, Agriculture-based	5.4	6.0	7.5	6.1	4.1	3.7	3.1	3.6	78	22	145	2	-38	-9
Relatively Industrialised Countries, Mineral-based	4.0	7.1	8.7	6.2	4.0	3.8	3.1	3.6	78	22	76	24	-13	13
Less Industrialised Countries, Agriculture-based	5.7	-1.4	4.3	2.5	2.5	-1.5	0.4	0.1	11	89	196	-47	-69	20
Less Industrialised Countries, Mineral-based	5.1	7.0	n.a.	6.1(b)	4.0	0.6	n.a.	0.9(b)	47	53	-3	-55	89	69
Least Developed Countries	6.4	2.2	9.0	5.2	5.1	0.4	4.2	2.7	73	27	128	-67	28	11
South Asia	2.7	1.8	3.0	2.4	8.3	2.8	2.8	4.0	80	20	170	-16	-57	3

Notes: (a) Average for 1974-78 except for less industrialised, mineral-based economies where data for 1978 are not available.

(b) Average for 1974-77.

TABLE I-4

DOMESTIC EXPENDITURE SHARES AND GNP GROWTH RATES IN SEVEN NON-OPEC DEVELOPING COUNTRY GROUPS(1)

	1963-73	1970-73	1973-76	1976-79	1973-79	1963-73	1970-73	1973-76	1976-79	1973-79	1963-73	1970-73	1973-76	1976-79	1973-79	1963-73	1970-73	1973-76	1976-79	1973-79
	Newly industrialising countries					Relatively industrialised countries with economies based predominantly on agriculture					Relatively industrialised countries with economies based predominantly on mineral-production					Less industrialised countries with economies based predominantly on agriculture				
Domestic Expenditure Shares(2) (per cent of GDP, in current prices)																				
Private Consumption	67.8	67.1	67.5	66.7	67.0	70.4	68.8	69.3	65.6	67.4	71.3	72.2	70.6	72.8	71.7	70.9	67.8	69.7	65.3	67.5
Public Consumption	10.7	10.7	11.4	11.9	11.6	12.7	13.9	12.9	14.2	13.5	12.3	13.8	13.1	14.0	13.6	14.3	15.0	14.4	13.6	14.0
Total Consumption	78.5	77.8	78.9	78.4	78.6	83.1	82.7	82.2	79.8	80.9	83.6	86.0	83.7	86.9	85.3	85.2	82.8	84.1	78.9	81.5
Gross Domestic Fixed Investment	21.9	23.0	24.7	23.8	24.2	16.9	17.4	20.8	21.8	21.3	15.7	14.5	15.7	14.7	15.2	16.0	17.5	17.7	20.1	18.9
Increase in Stocks	2.2	1.9	2.9	1.7	2.3	1.6	1.5	3.2	2.4	2.8	1.0	1.1	1.9	0.6	1.2	1.0	0.8	1.8	0.6	1.2
Gross Domestic Investment	24.1	24.9	27.6	25.5	26.5	18.5	18.9	24.0	24.2	24.1	16.7	15.6	17.6	15.3	16.4	17.0	18.3	19.5	20.7	20.1
Net Foreign Investment	-2.6	-2.7	-6.5	-3.9	-5.1	-1.6	-1.6	-6.2	-4.0	-5.0	-0.3	-1.6	-1.3	-2.1	-1.7	-2.2	-1.1	-3.6	0.4	-1.6
GNP Growth Rates (per cent)	7.3	8.3	4.5	5.1	4.7	5.8	6.8	7.3	5.6	6.6	4.5	3.9	1.6	4.0	2.8	4.0	3.3	1.1	5.5	3.3
	Less industrialised countries with economies based predominantly on mineral production					Least Developed Countries					South Asia									
Domestic Expenditure Shares(2) (per cent of GDP, in current prices																				
Private Consumption	56.6	54.3	54.3	59.8	57.1	74.5	73.5	74.8	72.5	73.6	78.3	78.7	79.5	73.9	76.7					
Public Consumption	17.6	20.3	20.1	19.8	19.9	13.5	14.6	14.0	13.9	14.0	9.2	9.9	9.0	9.8	9.4					
Total Consumption	74.2	74.6	74.4	79.6	77.0	88.0	88.1	88.8	86.4	87.6	87.5	88.6	88.4	83.7	86.0					
Gross Domestic Fixed Investment	21.4	25.8	24.5	25.2	24.9	13.9	13.9	14.3	16.1	15.2	16.0	15.1	15.9	19.0	17.0					
Increases in Stocks	1.9	2.9	4.0	2.0	3.0	0.7	1.0	3.0	0.9	1.9	2.0	2.7	3.9	2.8	3.8					
Gross Domestic Investment	23.3	28.7	28.5	27.2	27.9	14.6	14.9	17.3	17.0	17.1	18.0	18.8	19.8	21.8	20.8					
Net Foreign Investment	2.5	-3.3	-2.9	-6.8	-4.9	-2.6	-3.0	-6.1	-3.4	-4.7	-5.5	-7.4	-8.1	-5.5	-6.8					
GNP Growth Rates (per cent)	6.7	4.4	1.2	-0.8	0.0	3.8	3.2	2.4	1.7	2.2	3.6	1.3	4.5	4.2	4.6					

Sources: See Annex C.

Notes: (1) For coverage, see Annex B.

(2) Expenditure shares on average for the periods 1964-73, 1971-73, 1974-75, 1976-77, and 1974-77 for Chile and Brazil, private consumption includes increases in stocks.

Chapter II

THE ANALYTICAL FRAMEWORK

by Bela Balassa

1. EXTERNAL SHOCKS, POLICY RESPONSES AND INTERNAL SHOCKS

Introduction

Chapter I summarised the principal conclusions of the investigation and drew the implications of these conclusions for the policy response to the second oil shock of 1979-80. The analytical framework, employed to measure the balance-of-payments effects of external shocks, of policy reactions to these shocks, and of internal policy shocks, will be described in this Chapter, following a discussion of alternative policies that may be taken in response to, or independently from, external shocks.

The analytical framework will be applied to nine non-OPEC developing countries in Chapter III and to seven country groupings in Chapter IV. The relevant equations are shown in Annex A. Annex B contains a typology of the non-OPEC developing countries.

External Financing

Increased reliance on external financing by countries suffering unfavourable external shocks may involve increased borrowing abroad, a rise in foreign aid, increased foreign direct investment, or drawing down reserves. In turn, countries benefiting from favourable external shocks may reduce reliance on foreign borrowing, experience a decrease in foreign aid, discourage foreign direct investment, or accumulate reserves.

Foreign borrowing may be undertaken by the government itself, by public and parapublic agencies, or by private firms. In the last case, the government may also play a role in encouraging or discouraging foreign borrowing. Foreign borrowing may take the form of suppliers' credits, short-term borrowing from commercial banks and in the Euro-dollar market, and medium and long-term borrowing, usually from a consortium of banks, or through the issue of obligations in the Euro-bond market.

A developing country may also borrow from the World Bank, from regional development banks, or make drawings from the IMF. If such loans are provided at less than market rates, foreign borrowing will have a grant element. In turn, foreign aid may require eventual reimbursement, in part or in full, in which case it represents a mixture of foreign grants and foreign borrowing. In balance-of-payments statistics, however, the distinction is between foreign borrowing and foreign aid (official transfers), without regard to the terms of the loan or foreign aid.

In the case of loans on commercial terms, the interest rate, or rather, the premium paid above LIBOR (the London Interbank Rate), is determined by the country's creditworthiness. In evaluating creditworthiness, account is taken of factors such as the country's debt service obligations, usually related to the value of exports, its indebtedness, customarily expressed as a proportion of GNP, the availability or resources, and policies followed, when the "seal of good housekeeping" by the IMF will often play a role.

In appraising a policy of increased foreign borrowing, one needs to consider the extent to which the proceeds of the loan have been used to increase domestic consumption or investment, as well as the economic effectiveness of the investments undertaken. The former may be gauged by changes in the relative shares of consumption and investment in the gross domestic product, while an indication of the latter may be provided by the use of incremental capital-output ratios, supplemented by direct information on the efficiency of major investments.

Foreign direct investment may respond to investment incentives in the form of tax and credit preferences and is further affected by the administrative procedures applied. The economic efficiency of foreign investments will also depend on policies of import protection and export subsidisation that create a wedge between private and social profitability. In extreme cases, privately profitable investments in highly protected industries may involve a net loss of foreign exchange, resulting in negative social profitability, as the saving of foreign exchange through import substitution is exceeded by foreign exchange expenditure on materials and machinery, and the payment of dividends.

Finally, a country may draw down its reserves in the form of foreign exchange, gold and SDRs. However, countries may endeavour to maintain a minimum ratio between foreign indebtedness and reserves, possibly leading to parallel increases in both.

Export Promotion and Import Substitution

A neutral instrument of export promotion and import substitution is the exchange rate, inasmuch as a devaluation (appreciation) will increase (reduce) the profitability of traded goods vis-à-vis non-traded goods. The extent of devaluation or appreciation in real terms is indicated by the real exchange rate, calculated by adjusting changes in nominal exchange rates for changes in relative prices at home and abroad.

Export subsidies may take a variety of forms, including direct subsidies, preferential credits, and tax benefits, whereas traditional exports may be subject to taxes. In turn, measures of import protection include tariffs and tariff-type measures, such as import surcharges and advance deposits on imports, as well as quantitative restrictions in the form of quotas and import licensing.

The profitability of exports and import substitution is also affected by production subsidies and by price control. Finally, the government may undertake export-promoting and import-substituting investments directly, rather than promoting such investments by the use of incentive measures.

Macroeconomic Policies

For a devaluation to be effective, it needs to be supplemented by appropriate macroeconomic policy measures. Such measures may also be taken independently of exchange rate changes, with a view to reducing (or increasing) the rate of aggregate expenditure and hence, the rate of economic activity.

It is customary to distinguish between fiscal and monetary policy measures. But fiscal policies will also have monetary effects, either because budgetary deficits are financed through money creation or because they impinge on financial markets. In the latter case, the availability of capital for private investment is reduced. Private investment and consumption may also decline as a result of increased taxation.

While unfavourable external shocks may be met by deflationary macroeconomic policies, favourable external shocks permit the application of expansionary policies. But expansionary policies undertaken in the absence of favourable external shocks may themselves constitute an internal shock, leading to the deterioration in the balance of payments.

The choice of Countries and Country Groups

In the present investigation, the analytical framework has been applied to nine countries and to seven country groupings[1].

Among the individual countries under study, Brazil, Korea, Mexico and Portugal belong to the grouping of newly industrialising countries defined to include countries where the share of manufacturing in the gross domestic product exceeded 25 per cent and manufactured goods accounted for at least 50 per cent of exports in1973. In turn, Colombia, Malaysia, Peru and Tunisia are relatively industrialised developing countries, with the share of manufacturing in GDP between 15 and 25 per cent in 1973, the exception being Tunisia where this share was 11 per cent.

Among the four countries, the economies of Colombia and Malaysia are predominantly agricultural, with agriculture accounting for more than 25 per cent of GDP, and agricultural and related products providing over

1. See pages 8/9 for a description of the "ex post" country classification and pages 12/13 for the "ex ante" country-group typology.

50 per cent of exports. The economies of Peru and Tunisia are predominantly based on the production of minerals, which accounted for at least 10 per cent of GDP, and together with related products, provided 50 per cent or more of exports.

Finally, the Ivory Coast is classified among less industrialised developing countries whose economies are predominantly agricultural, with the share of agriculture in the gross domestic product exceeding 25 per cent and that of manufacturing varying between 10 and 15 per cent in 1973, and agricultural and related products providing at least 50 per cent of exports. The last three catagories are not represented in the sample of nine countries.

Alternatively, one may classify the nine countries according to their gross national product, population and GNP per capita. In 1973, Portugal was the only country in the group with per capita incomes in excess of $ 1,000; Mexico and Brazil had incomes between $ 800 and $ 900; Tunisia and Malaysia between $ 600 and $ 700; Colombia and the Ivory Coast between $ 400 and $ 500; and Korea and Peru between $ 300 and $ 400. By 1979, however, Korea assumed fourth place behind Mexico, which was surpassed by Brazil. Malaysia moved ahead of Tunisia and the Ivory Coast surpassed Colombia.

In terms of population, Brazil leads, followed by Mexico, Korea, Colombia, Peru, Malaysia, Portugal, the Ivory Coast and Tunisia; this order did not change between 1973 and 1979. But the order shown in 1973 in terms of the gross national product (Brazil, Mexico, Korea, Portugal, Colombia, Peru, Malaysia, Tunisia and the Ivory Coast) changed by 1979, as Colombia surpassed Portugal, Malaysia moved ahead of Peru, and the Ivory Coast surpassed Tunisia. Note, however, that these comparisons are subject to error, as they have been made at current exchange rates, which may have been over-or undervalued in the years 1973 or 1979.

TABLE II-1

GNP, Population and per capita - GNP of nine countries 1973-1979

Country	Gross National Product ($ billion)		Population (million)		Per Capita GNP (dollar)	
	1973	1979	1973	1979	1973	1979
Brazil	80.6	207.3	100.6	122.9	802	1687
Korea	13.1	55.9	34.1	37.3	385	1501
Tunisia	3.7	6.9	5.4	6.2	672	1113
Mexico	49.6	107.6	56.2	67.6	883	1592
Peru	9.2	12.5	14.6	17.3	339	723
Portugal	11.5	21.3	9.0	9.9	1280	2157
Colombia	10.0	26.4	22.3	26.1	447	1010
Ivory Coast	2.5	8.6	6.2	8.1	404	1060
Malaysia	7.4	18.0	11.3	13.7	650	1316

The estimates for the individual countries have been made for the years 1974 to 1977. For each individual year, the calculations refer to changes as compared to the average for the years 1971-73, denoted as "1972". Changes between individual years may be derived as the difference between the reported estimates for consecutive years. The tables further show averages of the estimates for the recession years 1974 and 1975, for the recovery years of 1976 and 1977, as well as for averages of all four years. For the seven country groupings, estimates for 1978 have also been made, the exception being the less industrialised mineral based countries, for which the relevant data were not available.

2. ESTIMATING THE BALANCE-OF-PAYMENTS EFFECTS OF EXTERNAL SHOCKS

Introduction

The effects of external shocks on the balance of payments of the countries and country groupings under study have been estimated by postulating a situation that would have occurred in the absence of these shocks.

In so doing, separate consideration has been given to the balance-of-payments impact of changes in the terms of trade (terms-of-trade effects) and the slowdown in foreign demand (export volume effects).

Terms-of-Trade Effects

In estimating the terms-of-trade effects of external shocks, the average for the years 1972-73 has been taken as a basis. It may be objected that, due to the effects of the world boom of 1972-73, the terms of trade of the developing countries were particularly favourable in 1971-73. However, the observed differences, as compared to the 1960s, were small and, in fact, the terms of trade of the developing countries were slightly less favourable in 1971-73 than in the 1960s if we exclude fuels, the prices of which started to rise in late 1973[1].

In making estimates for individual countries, changes in the terms of trade, relative to the 1971-73 base period, have been attributed to external shocks. The underlying assumption is that non-OPEC developing countries are price takers in world markets; i.e. world market prices are determined independently of actions taken by individual countries and of events, such as weather or strikes, which affect their production of particular commodities.

The assumption that, for individual countries, the world market prices of imports are given is applicable to all non-OPEC developing countries. This assumption also applies *grosso modo* to the principal exports of the countries studied, exceptions being coffee in Brazil and Colombia and rubber, palm oil, and tin in Malaysia. Nevertheless, in the absence of the explicit modelling of the world markets of these commodities, the assumption has been retained throughout.

Terms-of-trade effects have been calculated by revaluing imports and exports in the average prices of the years 1971-73 ("1972"), and taking the difference between **current-price** values and the **constant-price** values thereby obtained. They have further been decomposed into a pure terms-of-trade effect, estimated under the assumption of balanced trade in terms of "1972" prices, and the effects of the rise in import prices on unbalanced trade (the deficit or surplus in the balance of trade, calculated in "1972" prices)[2].

In the event of unbalanced trade in terms of "1972" prices, then, the estimated terms-of-trade effects include the impact of increases in import prices on the trade surplus (deficit). The procedure applied reflects the assumption that, in the absence of external shocks, import prices would have remained unchanged during the period under consideration. The assumption of unchanged import prices for non-OPEC developing countries has the following rationale.

Although primary product prices rose rapidly during the 1971-73 world boom, historical experience indicates that such price increases are followed by a decline or, at least, by a flat price trend. Primary product prices, in turn, influence the prices of manufactured goods, and it may not be unreasonable to assume that the world economy would have experienced a return to the non-inflationary situation of the 1960s if the quadrupling of petroleum prices had not occurred. At any rate, the rapid rise in petroleum prices accounts for a substantial part of the increase in import prices during this period.

In order to indicate the impact of the quadrupling of petroleum prices on the terms of trade, the balance-of-payments effects of changes in the prices of fuel and non-fuel imports are separately shown in the tables[3]. Distinction has further been made among various export categories.

Among merchandise exports, separate calculations have been made for traditional export products, defined to include primary commodities that accounted for at least 1.5 per cent of merchandise exports in the country (or country group) concerned in 1971-73. Calculations have also been made for the exports of fuels (SITC class 3), non-traditional primary products (SITC classes 0,1,2,4 and 68, less traditional primary exports), and manufactured goods (SITC classes 5,6,7,8, less 68).

1. The relevant index numbers for 1971-73, reported in United Nations, **Monthly Bulletin of Statistics**, (Dec. 1971) and (June 1977), are 103 including, and 93 excluding, fuels on a 1970 basis; the comparable averages for the 1961-70 period are 101 and 98, respectively.
2. This decomposition can be indicated by an example. Assume that import and export prices rose by 50 per cent and 40 per cent, respectively, between "1972" and 1977 and that imports and exports, valued in "1972" prices, were $220 million and $200 million in the latter year. The estimated terms of trade effects will now be $30 million, with the (pure) terms-of-trade effects of balanced trade being $20 million and the effects of the rise of import prices on unbalanced trade $10 million. (For the relevant formulas, see Annex A.)
3. With respect to the country groupings, non-fuel imports have, in turn, been separated into food (SITC classes 0,1,22 and 4), other primary products [SITC classes 2 (minus 22) and 68], capital goods (SITC class 1), and other manufactured goods [SITC classes 5, 6 (minus 68), 8 and 9].

Apart from traditional primary exports that differ among countries and country groupings, the above commodity categories have been utilised in the case of all the countries and country groupings included in the investigation. Estimates have further been made for service items and private transfers, whenever these reached at least one-sixth of the merchandise exports of a particular country. This has been the case for tourism and private transfers in Portugal and Tunisia, for tourism and border transactions in Mexico, and for construction activity in Korea. Such items have been treated in the same way as merchandise exports throughout the investigation.

Export Volume Effects

In order to indicate the balance-of-payments effects of the slowdown in foreign demand for a country's export products, we have estimated the **trend** value of exports that would have occurred in the absence of external shocks. Trend values of merchandise exports have been derived on the assumptions that world exports of the country's traditional export products, taken individually, and developing countries' exports of fuels, non-traditional primary products, and manufactured goods grew at the same rate as in the 1963-73 period **and** that the country (or country group) concerned maintained its "1972" market share in these exports. The underlying assumption is that a developing country competes against all suppliers in the world market for its traditional primary exports while its non-traditional exports compete against those of other developing countries.[1].

In the case of service items and private transfers (chiefly, workers' remittances), trend values have been derived with respect to markets that together accounted for more than two-thirds of the country's export revenue from the items in question. They include France, Germany, the Netherlands, Spain, the United Kingdom and the United States in regard to tourism in Portugal, and Belgium, France, Germany, Italy, the Netherlands, Sweden and Switzerland in regard to tourism in Tunisia. As regards workers' remittance, the relevant countries are France and Germany for Portugal, and Belgium, France, Germany, Italy, Libya and the Netherlands for Tunisia. For tourism and border transactions in Mexico comparisons have been made with the United States. Finally, for Korean construction activity, Iran, Kuwait and Saudi Arabia have been considered as the relevant markets.

The effects of changes in foreign demand on the country's exports have been derived as the difference between the **trend** value of exports and the **hypothetical** value of exports, both estimated in terms of "1972" prices for each of the relevant products and product groups. Hypothetical exports have been estimated on the assumptions that the country's exports of its traditional primary products grew at the same rate as world exports; that its exports of fuels, other non-traditional primary products, and manufactured goods increased at the same rate as developing country exports; and that its exports of particular service items and workers' remittances rose at the same rate as world exports to its major markets between "1972" and the year for which calculations have been made. The calculations again reflect the assumption that the country in question maintained its "1972" market share during the period under consideration.

Measuring export volume effects for individual developing countries may seem to conflict with the "small country" assumption, according to which the countries under study cannot affect the prices of their export products. This conflict is more apparent than real, inasmuch as shifts in world demand in the course of the business cycle may affect each country's export volume and price, without the individual countries being able to influence the price at which they sell.

The effects of the business cycle on trade are indicated by annual data for the developed countries' GNP and their imports from the developing countries. This is the case for the imports of primary as well as manufactured products. At the same time, manufactured imports were also affected by changes in protectionist measures.

Correspondingly, in the case of manufactured products, a further distinction has been made between the effects of lower foreign GNP growth rates and the effects of changes in foreign income elasticities of import demand, which have been taken to reflect the impact of trade policy measures in the importing countries. For this purpose, we have calculated the **constant-income-elasticity** value of exports that would have been obtained if – for actually observed GNP growth rates abroad – foreign income elasticities of import demand has remained the same as in the 1963-73 period **and** if the country in question had maintained its "1972" share in these exports. Separate calculations have been made for the country's (and country group's) exports to developed, developing and centrally planned economies.

The difference between the **trend** value and the **constant-income-elasticity** value of exports has been taken to reflect the effects of the decline in GNP growth rates abroad while the difference between the **constant-income-elasticity** value and the **hypothetical** value of exports has been taken to express the effects of changes in foreign

1. See footnote 2, page 13.

income elasticities of import demand. At the same time it should be recognised that increases in imports were not solely demand-determined but were influenced by supply factors as well. The effects of supply factors could not be separated, however.

3. ESTIMATING THE EFFECTS OF POLICY RESPONSES

Introduction

For estimating the effects of policy measures taken in response to external shocks, we again had to postulate a situation that would have occurred in the absence of these shocks. This has been done for additional net external financing, export promotion, import substitution and the effects of changes in economic growth rates on imports, taken individually.

The estimation of the balance-of-payments effects of policy measures taken in response to external shocks involves an imputation, in the sense that deviation from the estimated values of the relevant variables in the absence of external shocks are attributed to the policy measures taken in response to these shocks. Yet, as noted above, domestic policy changes may have occurred independently of external shocks and may themselves constitute an "internal shock".

The methodology does not permit separation of the balance-of-payments effects of policy responses to external shocks from the effects of autonomous policy changes. Such distinctions necessarily become a matter of interpretation of the evidence available for the country concerned.

Additional Net External Financing

The amount of additional net external financing has been estimated as the difference between the **actual** resource gap and the **trend** value of the resource gap. The actual resource gap definition equals the amount of net external financing. In turn, the trend value of the resource gap has been calculated by combining the trend value of imports and exports with the actual net balance of non-factor services and private transfers. However, as noted earlier, in certain cases service items and private transfers have been treated in the same way as merchandise exports.

The procedure applied assumes that additional external financing was not constrained by borrowing limitations abroad. The assumption does not exclude the possibility that increased borrowing occurred at higher interest rates. At the same time, in adding interest payments and dividends to additional net external financing, one obtains the total external financing of the country concerned.

Export Promotion

The effects of export promotion have been represented by changes in exports associated with changes in the country's (or country group's) "1972" market share. This has been done by taking the difference between the constant-price value of **actual** and of **hypothetical** exports. Separate calculations have been made for traditional primary products taken individually, fuels, non-traditional primary products, and manufactured goods, as well as for selected service items and private transfers.

Import Substitution

Import substitution is defined as savings in imports associated with a decrease in the country's (country group's) income elasticity of import demand. It has been derived by taking the difference between the constant-price values of **hypothetical** and **actual** imports, when the former has been obtained by combining actual GNP growth rates with income elasticities of import demand estimated for the 1963-73 period. Separate calculations have been made for fuel and for non-fuel imports in the case of individual countries and for food, fuel, other primary products, capital goods and other manufactures in the case of country groupings.

Lowering Economic Growth Rates

The effects on imports of lower (higher) economic growth rates in the country concerned have been estimated as the difference between constant-price values of imports obtained by combining income elasticities of import demand estimated for the 1963-73 period with GNP growth rates observed in the 1963-73 period (the **trend** value of imports) and with actual GNP growth rates observed during the period under consideration (the **hypothetical** value of imports), respectively. Again, separate calculations have been made for categories.

It should be noted, however, that changes in export market shares and in the rate of economic growth may have been due to circumstances outside the country's control. Thus, a decrease (increase) in the country's export market share may also have occurred because of an acceleration (deceleration) of exports by competing suppliers. In turn, a fall in foreign demand for the country's export products may have contributed to a decline in its rate of economic growth. Again, the relevance of these cases to a particular country becomes a matter of interpretation.

Concluding Remarks

As noted above, the balance-of-payments effects of external shocks, of policy responses to these shocks, and of internal shocks, have been estimated by postulating a situation that would have occurred in the absence of external and internal shocks. This involves making assumptions about an "anti-monde" that would have been established without such shocks.

The creation of an "anti-monde" would ideally involve estimating a complete economic model. Such a model would also permit examination of the impact of particular policy instruments, such as regulation of the exchange rate and the money supply, on the balance of payments, which necessarily becomes a matter of interpretation in the present analytical framework.

Nevertheless, by reason of limitations of time and data, we had to forego building complete economic models in the present investigation. The difficulties of model building were particularly forbidding in the case of the seven country groupings, for which estimates are presented in Chapter IV.

Notwithstanding its simplicity, the analytical framework has proved to be useful in providing a consistent set of estimates of the balance-of-payments effects of external shocks and of domestic policies. It has thus permitted indicating the relative importance of external shocks through the deterioration of the terms of trade and the slowdown of world demand-enables and of the various policy measures to be indicated.

Chapter III

THE BALANCE-OF-PAYMENTS EFFECTS OF EXTERNAL SHOCKS AND OF POLICY RESPONSES IN NINE NON-OPEC DEVELOPING COUNTRIES

by Bela Belassa

1. THE BALANCE-OF-PAYMENTS EFFECTS OF EXTERNAL SHOCKS

Introduction

Section 1 of this Chapter will present empirical evidence on the balance-of-payments impact of external shocks, in the form of terms-of-trade effects and export volume effects, in nine non-OPEC developing countries. Under each heading, the discussion will proceed by separating countries into three groups; it will be followed by a comparative analysis of external shocks in all nine countries.

As noted in Chapter I, the first group includes Brazil, Korea and Tunisia, all of which suffered adverse external shocks during the period under consideration. The second group of countries, comprising Mexico, Peru and Portugal, suffered adverse external shocks but also experienced internal shocks. In the third group of countries including Colombia, the Ivory Coast and Malaysia, external shocks were on balance favourable.

Table III-1A reports the estimated terms-of-trade and export volume effects for each of the years 1974 to 1977, together with averages for the years 1974-75, 1976-77 and 1974-77; more detailed results are shown in Appendix Table A-III-1.

Table III-1B relates terms of trade effects to the average value of trade and to the gross national product, and export volume effects to exports and to the gross national product, all expressed in terms of "1972" prices. Export volume effects are shown in a four commodity-group breakdown in Appendix Table A-III-2.

Terms of Trade Effects

Group I

Among the countries of the first group, Brazil and Korea suffered a substantial deterioration in their terms of trade in 1974, amounting to 49 per cent of the average value of exports and imports in both cases. The principal factor contributing to the deterioration in the terms of trade in the two countries was the quadrupling of petroleum prices, while increases in the prices of their non-oil imports and exports were nearly in balance.

Given its higher trade share, the ratio of the terms of trade loss to GNP was substantially larger in Korea (12.3 per cent) than in Brazil (3.3 per cent) in1974. These ratios remained unchanged in 1975, but declined in 1976 and in 1977 as Brazil benefited from increases in the prices of coffee and soybeans among its principal traditional exports and Korea, from higher prices of its manufactured exports. In 1977, the ratio was 0.7 per cent in Brazil and 1.3 per cent in Korea; for the period as a whole, it averaged 2.4 per cent and 7.7 per cent in the two countries, respectively.

As noted in Chapter II, the terms-of-trade loss may be decomposed into two parts. a pure terms-of-trade effect, calculated on the assumption of balanced trade in terms of "1972" prices, and the effects on the rise in import prices on unbalanced trade. In the 1974-77 period, on the average, pure terms of trade effects accounted for 47 per cent of the total in Brazil and 87 per cent in Korea. Both of these components were affected to a considerable extent by the rise in petroleum prices.

The pattern of terms of trade changes was very different in Tunisia which had small net exports of petroleum. With the price of one of its principal exports, phosphates, quadrupling between "1972" and 1974, Tunisia showed a net terms of trade gain in 1974. This gain subsequently turned into a loss as the price of phosphates fell by one-half between 1974 and 1977. The effects of higher import prices on Tunisia's trade deficit, expressed in terms of "1972" prices, fully accounted for this loss.

Group II

In the second group, Portugal suffered the smallest terms-of-trade loss, amounting to 15.7 per cent of the average value of exports and imports and 3.5 per cent of GNP in 1974, largely because of favourable developments in the prices of its tourist services and workers' remittances. Portugal's terms-of-trade loss increased in subsequent years as the prices of most of its traditional exports declined. This loss reached 34.7 per cent of the average value of trade and 7.3 per cent of GNP in 1977; for the years 1974-77, on average, the corresponding ratios were 27.3 per cent and 5.6 per cent. The pure terms-of-trade effect represented three-fourths of the loss.

The increase in the absolute value of imports due to the rise in import prices was the same in Mexico as in Portugal in 1974. Mexico also experienced favourable developments in the prices of its tourist services and border transactions[1] so that the terms-of-trade loss amounted to only 9.1 per cent of the average value of its exports and imports in that year. Given its substantially smaller trade share, the loss equalled 0.7 per cent of Mexico's GNP.

Following a deterioration in 1975, the situation improved in subsequent years, largely as a result of the gain accruing to Mexico from higher prices on its rising petroleum exports and tourists services. By 1977, Mexico enjoyed a small net gain from terms-of-trade changes. Its terms-of-trade loss was 6.8 per cent of the average value of trade and 0.5 per cent of GNP in the years 1974-77, on average. This loss was largely due to the impact of increased import service on Mexico's trade deficit, estimated in "1972" prices, as the pure terms-of-trade effect, calculated on the assumption of balanced trade in terms of "1972" prices, were negligible.

Peru's terms of trade loss amounted to 24.2 per cent of the average value of its exports and imports and 3.9 per cent of its GNP in 1974. With the decline by over one-third in the price of copper, its principal export product, Peru's terms of trade deteriorated further in 1975, with only a slight improvement in 1976 and in 1977.

In 1977, the terms-of-trade loss amounted to 65.5 per cent of the average value of trade and 9.9 per cent of GNP in Peru. For the years 1974-77, on average, the corresponding figures were 61.3 per cent and 9.1 per cent. In the same period, the pure terms-of-trade effect accounted for one-fourth of the loss; the remainder was due to the effects of rising import prices on Peru's trade deficit.

Group III

Countries of the third group enjoyed considerable terms of trade gains during the period under consideration. In the years 1974-77, on average, this gain amounted to 26.9 per cent of the average value of exports and imports in the Ivory Coast, 24.0 per cent in Malaysia, and 15.7 per cent in Colombia; given differences in trade shares, the ratio of the gain to GNP was 9.3 per cent in the Ivory Coast, 7.8 per cent in Malaysia and 1.2 per cent in Colombia.

Colombia and Malaysia had an export surplus in fuels in 1974, and hence, benefited from rising petroleum prices. But while this surplus increased over time in Malaysia, it gave place to a small deficit in Colombia. In turn, the Ivory Coast continued to import the bulk of its energy needs during the period under consideration.

All three countries benefited, however, from increases in the prices of their traditional primary exports in 1976 and in 1977. As a result, they experienced rising terms-of-trade gains after a small loss in 1975, which had followed a gain in 1974 (Colombia excepted). Colombia and the Ivory Coast benefited from the rise in the price of coffee in 1976 that continued in 1977; the Ivory Coast further enjoyed an increase in the price of cocoa during this period. The rising prices of rubber and tin provided the bulk of Malaysia's term-of-trade gain in both 1976 and 1977.

In the Ivory Coast and Malaysia, the pure terms-of-trade effect accounted for two-thirds of the terms of trade gain in the years 1974-77, on average; the remainder is explained by the fact that increases in import prices

1. Border transactions are shown under private transfers in Appendix A-III-1.

magnified the surplus in the balance of trade of the two countries, expressed in "1972" prices. In turn, the pure terms-of-trade effect had to compensate for the effects of higher import prices on Colombia's small trade deficit.

Export Volume Effects

Group I

In 1974, the slowdown in foreign demand gave rise to an export shortfall amounting to 3.7 per cent of export value in Brazil, 3.6 per cent in Korea, and 7.3 per cent in Tunisia, expressed in terms of "1972" prices[1]. In the case of Korea, the relatively favourable results are explained by the high share of manufactured exports (84 per cent in "1972"), for which foreign demand did not turn down until late 1974. The share of manufactured goods in total exports was smaller in Brazil (14 per cent) which benefited however from continued strong demand for soybeans, oilcake, and iron ore among its traditional primary exports.

In subsequente years, demand for the exports of Brazil and Korea largely paralleled the world business cycle, with the export shortfall increasing in 1975, declining in 1976, and rising again in 1977, when it reached a level substantially higher than that experienced in 1974. Similar developments were observed in Tunisia, except that an improvement in 1976 did not occur.

In the years 1974-77, on average, export volume effects amounted to 8.2 per cent of export value in Brazil, 7.7 per cent in Korea, and 15.2 per cent in Tunisia. The larger shortfall in the case of Tunisia is explained by unfavourable trends in tourism, in foreign demand for its labour, and in world demand for its traditional exports, in particular olive oil, which declined by over one-fourth between "1972" and 1977. Tunisia's higher trade share further magnified the ratio of its export shortfall to GNP in Tunisia (3.6 per cent in the years 1974-77, on average) as compared to Brazil (0.4 per cent), with Korea occupying an intermediate position (2.4 per cent). In Korea, relatively favourable demand conditions for its manufactured exports mitigated the effects of adverse changes in world demand for its traditional primary products.

Group II

In 1974, adverse export volume effects were concentrated in tourism in Portugal, amounting to 3.9 per cent of export value and 0.8 per cent of GNP. In subsequent years, export shortfalls in manufactured goods and worker's remittances assumed importance, due largely to the decline in the growth of demand for manufactured imports and labour in Western Europe. Export shortfalls amounted to 32.2 per cent of exports and 6.1 per cent of GNP in 1977; the corresponding ratios for the years 1974-77, on average, were 19.9 per cent and 3.9 per cent.

Due to continued rapid increases in world demand for its traditional exports, in particular copper, export volume effects in Peru were favourable in 1974. These effects turned negative, however, in 1975, when demand for Peru's traditional exports declined. A further deterioration occurred in 1976, followed by improvements in 1977. For the years 1974-77, on average, the export shortfall amounted to 18.6 per cent of the value of exports and 2.3 per cent of GNP. Throughout the period, the observed changes were largely determined by changes in world demand for copper.

In Mexico, export volume effects were slightly favourable in1974 as gains in border transactions exceeded losses in merchandise trade. The situation deteriorated in subsequent years with increasing losses in border transactions; by 1977, the shortfall reached 17.8 per cent of exports and 1.3 per cent of GNP. The average ratio for the period as a whole was 10.1 per cent of exports and 0.7 per cent of GNP.

Group III

In the countries of the third group, which experienced favourable terms-of-trade effects during the period under consideration, adverse export volume effects were largely concentrated in traditional primary exports. Except for sugar, world demand was lower in 1974 than in "1972" for all of Colombia's traditional exports; in the case of the Ivory Coast, similar results were obtained for coffee, cocoa beans, bananas, and cotton; while Malaysia experienced a decline only in the world demand for tin.

With world demand for its other traditional exports continuing to grow, albeit at a reduced rate, the adverse export volume effects accounted for a smaller proportion of export value in1977 in Malaysia (15.1 per cent) than

1. It should be recalled that changes between successive years are obtained as the difference between the estimates for the years in question.

in either the Ivory Coast (20.1 per cent) or in Colombia (25.1 per cent). Considering the period as a whole, however, the difference between Malaysia and Colombia was smaller (10.4 per cent vs 11.5 per cent) as Colombia experienced favourable trends in world demand for its traditional primary exports in the mid-seventies and further benefited from the expansion of demand for its manufactured exports in Latin America.

Among the countries of the group, the shortfall for the entire period was the largest in the Ivory Coast (14.1 per cent of exports), where low levels of world demand for cocoa, bananas and cotton were not compensated by increased demand for manufactured exports. Expressed as a proportion of GNP, the corresponding results were 0.9 per cent for Colombia, 3.6 per cent for Malaysia and 5.1 per cent for the Ivory Coast.

Comparative Analysis

In the third group of countries, the gain from terms of trade effects was approximately double the loss from export volume effects in the Ivory Coast and Malaysia and about 40 per cent higher in Colombia in the years 1974-77, on average. The difference in effects was even larger in 1977, when terms-of-trade gains were about three times the export volume shortfalls in all the countries of this group.

Apart from Tunisia, which had an export surplus in fuels during the period under consideration, the adverse terms-of-trade effects dominated the export volume effects in the first group of countries. In 1974, the ratio of the former to the latter was 17.5 in Brazil and 15.2 in Korea. Among the countries of the second group, the ratio was 4.1 in Portugal while Peru experienced favourable export volume effects.

The ratio of terms-of-trade effects to export volume effects fell over time in Brazil, Korea and Portugal. Notwithstanding fluctuations paralleling the business cycle, the adverse export volume effects increased in all three countries while the loss from terms-of-trade effects declined in Brazil and in Korea and increased relatively slowly in Portugal.

Terms-of-trade effects, however, continued to exceed export volume effects by a substantial margin in Brazil, Korea, and Portugal, all of which suffered the adverse effects of the quadrupling of petroleum prices. This conclusion also applies to Peru where the export volume effects turned unfavourable in 1975 but remained less than one-half of the terms-of-trade effects throughout the period. Finally, Mexico represents a special case, inasmuch as high prices for its newly-developed petroleum exports and for tourist services reduced the terms-of-trade loss below the export shortfall.

The result show the importance of the rise in petroleum prices and conflict with the conventional wisdom that gives emphasis to the unfavourable effects of the 1974-75 world recession and the subsequent slow recovery on the developing countries' balance of payments. Nor does one find evidence of the alleged adverse effects of increased protectionism on the developing countries' exports of manufactured goods. As the estimates reported in Appendix Table A-III-1 indicate, the foreign income elasticity of demand for the manufactured exports of these countries was higher during the period under consideration than in the previous decade, offsetting in part the unfavourable effects of lower GNP growth rates abroad. And while the observed changes were significantly affected by efforts made in the developing countries to expand and diversify export supply, these efforts would not have borne fruit without market possibilities abroad.

For most non-OPEC developing countries, data on manufactured exports are available in a geographical breakdown. The data show that in the developed countries, which continued to provide markets for the bulk of the developing countries' manufactured exports, increases in the income elasticity of demand for these products offset about one-fifth of the export shortfall due to their lower GNP growth rates. In centrally planned economies, declines in the income elasticity of demand for the manufactured exports of the developing countries aggravated the adverse effects of lower GNP growth rates. In intra-LDC trade, the increase in the income elasticity of demand reinforced the favourable effects of higher GNP growth rates.

2. THE POLICIES APPLIED AND THEIR BALANCE-OF-PAYMENTS EFFECTS

Introduction

Section 1 has analysed the impact of external shocks, in the form of terms-of-trade effects and export volume effects, on the balance of payments of nine non-OPEC developing countries, classified into three groups. Section 2 will examine the policies applied in the three groups of countries and indicate the balance-of-payments effects of these policies. It will further present estimates of the balance-of-payments impact of additional net external financing, export promotion, import substitution, and lowering the rate of economic growth in these countries in the years 1974-77, on average, and provide a comparative analysis of the results.

The balance-of-payments effects of the policies applied in the individual countries are shown in Table III-1A while Table III-1B relates the results to the volume of exports, imports, average trade, and GNP, as the case may be, all expressed in "1972" prices. More detailed estimates are given in Appendix Tables A-III-1 and A-III-2. Information is further provided on the financing of the resource gap in Table III-2, on changes in nominal and real interest rates and the government budget in Table III-3, and on nominal and real exchange rates in Table III-4.

In interpreting the results, it should be recalled that additional net external financing is estimated as the difference between the actual resource gap – or net external financing (the actual net balance of goods, nonfactor services, and private transfers) – and its trend value (the difference between the trend values of imports and exports, both expressed in "1972" prices, adjusted for the actuel net balance of non-factor services and private transfers). In turn, total external financing is the sum of net external financing, interest payments, and dividends.

The rise in exports associated with increases in market shares is deemed to reflect the effects of export promotion. It is measured as the difference between actual exports and hypothetical exports, the latter being calculated on the assumption that the country in question maintained its export market share[1]. In turn, import substitution and the effects of changes in GNP growth rates, are estimated as the difference between hypothetical and actual imports, and between trend and hypothetical imports, respectively, where trend imports are derived by assuming the continuation of import growth rates observed in the 1963-73 period, and hypothetical imports are calculated by combining the income elasticities of import demand observed in the 1963-73 period with actual GNP growth rates.

The Policies Applied

Group I

In 1974-75, on average, the combined balance-of-payments effects of external shocks, associated with changes in the terms of trade and in foreign demand, amounted to 3.7 per cent of GNP in Brazil, 14.5 per cent in Korea, and 0.9 per cent in Tunisia. The corresponding figures for 1976-77 were 2.1 per cent for Brasil, 6.5 per cent for Korea, and 9.0 per cent for Tunisia.

In **Brazil**, the immediate response to external shocks was to increase foreign borrowing to maintain high rates of economic growth. In the years 1974-75, the deterioration in the balance of payments due to external shocks was fully financed from abroad. At the same time, increases in export market shares were offset by the rise in imports associated with higher GNP growth rates, and import substitution was practically nil.

Apart from permitting continued increases in domestic consumption, the amounts borrowed were employed to finance large investments in infrastructure and in import-substituting industries producing intermediate goods. These investments were undertaken in the framework of the Second National Development Plan, which called for large investments in pulp and paper, petrochemicals, fertilizer, steel, and nonferrous metals, with the objective of reaching or of approaching self-sufficiency by 1979.

In turn, capital goods industries were promoted by a combination of import restrictions, fiscal incentives, and credit preferences. Credit preferences increased in scope after 1973 while real interest rates turned negative. Apart from adverse effects on the efficient allocation of investment funds, negative real interest rates also reduced the incentive to save.

Various measures were used to limit imports, including an increase in tariffs, advance deposit requirements, and import restrictions. Notwithstanding the introduction of new export incentives, the net effect was to increase the bias against exports and in favour of import substitution. At the same time, the real value of the cruzeiro remained practically unchanged.

The application of these measures led to considerable import substitution while gains in exports, resulting from increases in market shares, declined, offsetting the import savings associated with the deceleration in economic growth. As import substitution came to exceed the combined balance-of-payments effects of external shocks

1. Comparison is made with world exports in the case of the countrys traditional primary exports, taken individually, with developing country exports in the case of the other major export product categories, and with world exports to major markets in the case of particular service items and worker remittances.

in 1976-77, reliance on additional foreign borrowing gave way to reserve accumulation, as actual net external financing ($1.6 billion) fell till the trend value of net external financing of $2.2 billion.

As far as 1976-77 is concerned, however, this should be viewed in the light of the increased burden of interest payments and dividends on Brazil's balance of payments. These payments amounted ot $1.0 billion in "1972", increased to $2.2 billion in 1974-75 and to $2.8 billion in 1976-77. By 1977, Brazil's total external financing requirements, inclusive of interest payments and dividends, reached $ 5.4 billion.

In 1977, Brazil was favoured by the high price of coffee; the situation changed in 1978, however when net external financing and total external financing, respectively, rose to $2.7 billion and to $7.6 billion, as the price of coffee declined. At the same time, with high cost, inefficient investments raising incremental capital-output ratios, the rate of growth of GNP declined.

Korea also increased reliance on foreign capital in response to the external shocks it suffered in 1974 and in 1975. It did not, however, bias the system of incentives against exports, but provided increased export incentives through preferential credit allocations. It also aided savings and investment through the application of investment incentives and re-established positive real interest rates after 1975. The resulting increase in investment shares more than offset the rise in incremental capital output ratios, leading to an acceleration of the GNP growth rate.

Correspondingly, Korea rapidly expanded production for export as well as for domestic markets. Notwithstanding the appreciation of the real exchange rate from its greatly undervalued 1973 level, in 1974-75 increases in export shares and import substitution, taken together, fully offset the adverse effects of external shocks on Korea's balance of payments. Additional net external financing, in turn, paid for the increased imports associated with higher GNP growth rates.

The Korean government undertook some measures of import liberalisation after 1975 and reduced tariffs in 1977, thereby improving relative incentives to exports. As a result, export expansion assumed increasing importance as compared to import substitution. Despite the further appreciation of the real exchange rate, these two effects combined came to exceed the adverse balance-of-payments effects of external shocks four-and-a-half times in 1976-77. Although higher GNP growth rates added $1.4 billion to the import bill, $1.2 billion in reserves were accumulated.

Actual net external financing was practically zero in Korea in 1977. In contrast to Brazil, rapid export expansion and import substitution permitted reducing foreign borrowing after 1975. And while the overheating of the economy, together with the further appreciation of the real exchange rate, necessitated increased external financing in 1978, total external financing of $2.3 billion in that year was still short of the level of $2.4 billion observed in both 1974 and 1975, although the gross national product had increased substantially in the meantime.

After favourable net external shocks in 1974 – due in part to the quadrupling of the price of phosphates – **Tunisia's** terms of trade turned unfavourable, thereby aggravating the effects of the rising export shortfall that resulted from adverse world market conditions. However, export promotion, which began in the early seventies, led to increases in export market shares, offsetting about two-thirds of the export shortfall.

At the same time, investment incentives, and an increase in investible funds associated with positive real interest rates after 1975, contributed to the rise in investment and led to an increased rate of economic growth as compared to the 1963-73 period. This rapid GNP growth and the import needs of investment, however, increased Tunisia's import bill, necessitating a substantial rise in additional net external financing.

The ratio of additional net external financing to GNP rose from 4.7 per cent in 1974-75, on average, to 16.4 per cent in 1976-77. It reached $0.6 billion in 1977, equivalent to 18.3 per cent of the gross national product, when the trend value of net external financing was $–0.1 billion. In the same year, the combined amount of interest payments and dividends hardly exceeded $0.1 billion, reflecting the fact that net external financing had been negligible in the years before 1975.

With an increase in foreign borrowing in subsequent years, however, interest payments and dividends rose by about one-half in 1978, when net external financing was $0.3 billion and total external financing, $0.5 billion.

Group II

After reaching a peak of $1.1 billion in 1975, the adverse effects of external shocks on **Mexico's** balance of payments declined to $0.7 billion (equivalent to 1.2 per cent of GNP) in 1977, when the terms-of-trade gain due to the higher prices of tourist services and of the rapidly increasing oil exports was $0.1 billion. There was a parallel decline in additional net external financing but it continued to exceed the balance-of-payments effects of external shocks throughout the period under consideration. This is because savings in imports, associated with lower GNP growth rates, did not suffice to offset the deterioration in the balance of payments resulting from decreases in export market shares and increases in import shares.

These changed trade shares show the direct and indirect effects of expansionary fiscal policies followed under the Echeverria Administration as of 1972. These policies entailed a rapid increase in government expenditure without a corresponding increase in revenue. As a result, the government budget deficit, expressed as a proportion of GNP, increased from 0.7 per cent in 1971 to 3.6 per cent in 1974; in the following two years, it was between 3.0 and 3.5 per cent of GNP. This deficit financed the expansion of current as well as capital expenditures. As the investment funds were not often productively used, incremental capital-output ratios increased and GNP growth rates declined during this period.

The budget deficit was financed by money creation and by foreign borrowing. Money creation gave rise to rapid inflation and to a deterioration in Mexico's competitiveness that is not fully reflected by real exchange rates calculated in reference to relative prices. This is because, in Mexico's relatively open economy, increases in wages could not be fully translated into higher prices.

The decline in Mexico's competitiveness was not offset by a devaluation until September 1976. The devaluation, and the restrictive policies adopted under the Administration of Lopez Portillo in 1977, led to improvements in export performance and to reductions in import shares. These changes were not sufficient, however, to undo the adverse effects of the policies followed in earlier years, so that losses in export market shares and increases in import shares were still observed in that year. Furthermore, expansionary policies were again adopted in 1978, when the budget deficit approached 5 per cent of GNP.

In Mexico, then, the effects of internal shocks in the form of expansionary policies overshadowed the effects of external shocks. And while, aided by the *deus ex machina* of petroleum exports, net external financing fell from its 1975 peak of $2.5 billion to practically nil in 1977 and in 1978, total external financing was still $2.3 billion in 1977 and increased again to $3.0 billion in 1978. This result was largely due to interest payments on debt contracted after 1971 to finance the growing balance-of-payments deficit associated with expansionary policies.

In **Portugal**, external shocks took the form of rising terms-of-trade losses and export shortfalls, while the internal shock was the revolution of April 1974. The political changes engendered a "revolution of rising expectations", leading to the rapid expansion of government spending as well as rapid increases in wages. Uncompensated by higher taxes, the expansion of government spending gave rise to a budget deficit amounting to 2.2 per cent of GNP in 1974, 5.4 per cent in 1975, and 7.0 per cent in 1976. Also, profit margins declined as wage increases could not be fully compensated by increases in prices, and disruptions in production reduced labour productivity.

The inflationary effects of government spending, declines in profit margins, and disruptions in production, together with the bias against exports associated with the application of import protection measures, led to losses in Portugal's market shares in merchandise exports to the developed countries. The resulting fall in exports was aggravated by the loss of markets in the former colonies that became independent in the wake of the revolution. Unsettled conditions following the revolution also had unfavourable effects on foreign tourism and on workers' remittances.

The loss in export market shares was offset in large part by decreases in imports associated with the deceleration of economic growth and, to a much lesser extent, import substitution. The deceleration of economic growth was largely the result of the revolution that occasioned an absolute fall in GNP in 1975, followed by a slow recovery. Import substitution, due to the imposition of protective measures, declined in later years as imports were liberalised.

With the effects of domestic policy measures on exports and imports nearly offsetting each other, additional net external financing slightly exceeded the balance-of-payments effects of external shocks in 1974-75 as well as in 1976-77. By 1977, additional net external financing had reached $1.7 billion, equivalent to 13.7 per cent of Portugal's GNP. However, actual net external financing was only $0.9 billion, reflecting the fact that continuation of the earlier surplus would have given rise to a (trend) capital inflow of $0.8 billion. With the deficit being financed largely by reserves, total external financing ($1.1 billion in 1977) exceeded net external financing by a relatively small margin.

Improvements in the balance of payments occurred in 1978 as a result of the restrictive monetary measures taken in late 1977 and mid-1978 as well as the application of a policy of wage restraint that permitted rebuilding profit margins. The results were quite immediate, with net external financing declining to $0.3 billion and total external financing falling to $0.7 billion in 1978.

In **Peru**, the net impact of external shocks was practically zero in 1974, as favourable export volume effects nearly offset the unfavourable terms-of-trade effects. The situation changed in 1975 when adverse developments occurred in both terms of trade and export-volume effects, largely because of the decline in foreign demand for, and the associated fall in the world market price of copper. The adverse balance-of-payments effects of external shocks reached 16.0 per cent of GNP in 1975, declining thereafter to 15.2 per cent in 1976 and to 13.3 per cent in 1977.

External shocks reinforced the adverse effects of internal shocks represented by the policies of the military regime of General Velasco, instituted in 1969. While – aided by favourable changes in the terms of trade – the rate of growth of GNP remained relatively high until 1973, the decline in the volume of export associated with the increasing overvaluation of the exchange rate, the chaotic economic management of state enterprises, and the fall in private investment in response to political and economic uncertainties created increasing economic difficulties. The difficulties were aggravated by the government budget deficit, which amounted to 3 to 4 per cent of GNP in the early seventies and reached 5.6 per cent of GNP in 1975. The deficit financed rising military expenditures and an ambitious programme of investments of often doubtful efficiency, which raised incremental capital-output ratios and adversely affected the rate of economic growth.

The appreciation of the real exchange rate aggravated the effect on the import bill of military expenditures and the public investment programme, giving rise to an increase in import shares in both 1974 and 1975. In turn, the decline in the anchovy catch reinforced the adverse effect on export earnings of the overvaluation of the exchange rate, resulting in losses in export market shares in 1974. And while increased fishmeal and copper exports led to a gain in market shares in 1975, this occurred only in comparison to the depressed exports of "1972". The export gain only partially compensated for the adverse balance-of-payments effects of import substitution that were further aggravated by increased imports associated with higher growth rates.

All in all, the negative balance-of-payments effects of domestic policies affecting exports, import substitution, and the rate of economic growth amounted to 5.6 per cent of GNP in 1974-75, on the average. With the adverse balance-of-payments effects of external shocks averaging 8.4 per cent, additional net external financing reached 14.0 per cent of GNP during this period. Given the relatively small negative trend value of the resource gap, actual net external financial requirements were only slightly lower, equalling 12.4 per cent of GNP. Despite rising foreign investment in copper and petroleum, Peru had to increasingly rely on foreign loans to finance its balance-of-payments deficit. Continued increases in foreign borrowing, in turn, raised questions about the country's creditworthiness.

The governement of General Bermudez, installed in August 1975, attempted to remedy the situation. In fact, improved business confidence, together with the depreciation of the real exchange rate, led to increases in export shares and reductions in import shares in 1976 and in 1977. However, the budget deficit continued to rise, reaching 6.4 per cent of GNP in 1976 and 7.6 per cent in 1977.

With the maintenance of expansionary policies and reductions in foreign direct investment, the balance-of-payments effects of external shocks necessitated drawing down reserves and continued foreign borrowing. In 1976-77, additional net external financing averaged $0.9 billion, equivalent to 10.9 per cent of GNP, while actual net external financing was $0.7 billion and total external financing, augmented by rising interest payments and dividends, was $1.4 billion.

Peru's balance-of-payments situation improved substantially as a result of the May 1978 policy package, (which included a large devaluation, the adoption of the crawling peg, and restraint on government spending) as well as an increase in the prices of copper and petroleum exports. With the decline in GNP following the application of deflationary policies, Peru's resource gap turned positive in 1978, although interest payments of $0.5 billion gave rise to total external financing of $0.2 billion.

Group III

In **Colombia**, adverse external shocks, which averaged 1.4 per cent of GNP in 1974-75, gave place to positive effects (2.0 per cent of GNP) in 1976-77, as a result of the rapid increase in the price of coffee. The opportunity provided by the improvement in the balance of payments was not utilised, however, to accelerate the rate of growth of investment and of GNP. Rather, the rate of economic growth declined from 5.6 per cent between 1963 and 1973 to 4.7 per cent between 1973 and 1977, while the share of investment in GNP remained roughly the same. This outcome was the result of changes in the system of incentives that were undertaken in the wake of the coffee price boom.

To begin with, the authorities limited increases in interest rates and reduced the rate of crawl of the exchange rate, notwithstanding the acceleration of inflation occasioned by the rise in the money supply, as the credit measures taken did not suffice to offset the effects of the increase in foreign exchange reserves on domestic money holdings. The adverse effects on exports of the appreciation of the exchange rate in real terms were aggravated by the elimination of export subsidies.

With the increased bias against exports, Colombia experienced declines in its export market shares in manufactured goods. A loss in export shares was also observed in fuels, which was only partly offset by gains in traditional and non-traditional primary exports in the years 1976-77. Due to the appreciation of the real exchange rate and, to a lesser extent, measures of import liberalisation, Colombia also experienced increased import shares while growth effects on imports were negligible.

The negative balance-of-payments effects of domestic policies offset three-fourths of the favourable effects of positive external shocks in 1976-77, permitting an accumulation of $610 million in reserves, although interest and dividend payments on previous borrowing amounted to $340 million.

Due to parallel changes in their terms of trade, the balance-of-payments effects of external shocks showed a similar pattern in the **Ivory Coast** and in **Malaysia**. In both cases, favourable external shocks in 1974 gave way to adverse shocks in 1975, which were, in turn, followed by favourable shocks of increasing magnitude. In 1977, the balance-of-payments effects of favourable external shocks equalled 13.2 per cent of GNP in the Ivory Coast and 9.7 per cent in Malaysia.

Both the Ivory Coast and Malaysia increased their export market shares in primary, as well as in manufactured goods, during the period under consideration. Malaysia also experienced the effects of import substitution but these were more than offset by the effects of the acceleration of GNP growth on imports. In turn, the Ivory Coast increased its import shares which were partially offset by reductions in imports associated with the deceleration of economic growth. A variety of policy measures taken by the two countries contributed to these results.

The Ivory Coast enjoyed increases in export market shares – notwithstanding the appreciation of the real exchange rate -- following measures of export diversification taken in the early seventies, which encouraged the expansion of non-traditional primary and manufactured exports. In manufacturing, the duty-free admission of imported inputs and the scaling-down of export tax rates at higher levels of fabrication were of particular importance.

The appreciation of the real exchange rate, however, contributed to increased import shares in the Ivory Coast, which were further aggravated by the import intensity of rising investment. A substantial part of new investment was undertaken in the framework of public investment programmes in highly capital-intensive industries. Correspondingly, rather than raising the rate of economic growth, increases in the investment effort were absorbed by higher incremental capital-output ratios.

Malaysia's exports were favourably affected by the depreciation of the exchange rate in real terms. Other factors contributing to export expansion found their origin in measures taken in the late sixties and early seventies. They include the oil-palm planting programme; the granting of logging and sawmilling licenses; and the policy of active exploration for petroleum with the participation of foreign companies.

The depreciation of the real exchange rate also contributed to import substitution and to increases in profit margins in Malaysia. The generation of investible funds by businesses and by private individuals, who continued to benefit from positive real interest rates, in turn, led to the rise in investment activity. With increased investment, economic growth accelerated, leading to higher import levels.

In both the Ivory Coast and Malaysia, the balance-of-payments effects of domestic policy measures affecting export promotion, import substitution, and the rate of economic growth were positive in the years 1976-77, on average. Correspondingly, savings in additional foreign borrowing exceeded the balance-of-payments impact of favourable external shocks in the two countries. Actual net external financing was, however, lower in the Ivory Coast, and higher in Malaysia, as the trend values of net external financing were positive in the first case and negative in the second. Also, interest payments and dividends resulted in positive total external financing in the Ivory Coast but in an outflow of capital in Malaysia. Finally, with the decline in the price of coffee in 1978, the Ivory Coast renewed reliance upon additional foreign borrowing, while Malaysia, with more diversified exports, did so only minimally.

Additional Net External Financing

Group I

In the 1974-77 period, on average, additional net external financing amounted to 23.5 per cent of the average value of exports and imports expresses in "1972" prices in Brazil, –23.7 per cent in Korea, and 44.3 per cent in Tunisia. But, given its much smaller trade share, the ratio of additional external financing to the average value of GNP, expressed in "1972" prices, was only 1.4 per cent in Brazil as compared to –6.7 per cent in Korea and 11.3 per cent in Tunisia.

The trend value of the resource gap in the years 1974-77, on average, was 16.3 per cent of Korea's GNP, reflecting the fact that its "1972" trade deficit would have increased further had export and import trends observed in the previous decade continued. Such was also the case, albeit to a much lesser extent, in Brazil where the trend value of the resource gap was estimated at 2.6 per cent of GNP. The opposite result was obtained in Tunisia, where the continuation of earlier trends would have given rise to an outflow of capital amounting to 2.8 per cent of GNP.

Correspondingly, the actual resource gap averaged 4.0 per cent of Brazil's GNP, expressed in terms of "1972" prices, during the 1974-77 period. Taking further account of interest payments and dividends, the ratio of total external financing to GNP was 6.7 per cent. Foreign borrowing provided nearly four-fifths of Brazil's total external financing requirements, with foreign direct investment accounting for another one-fifth. In the same period, there was a small accumulation of reserves.

In Korea, net external financing and total external financing averaged 7.6 per cent and 10.9 per cent of GNP, respectively, in the years 1974-77. Including errors and omission, which largely represented unreported short-term capital flows, foreign borrowing approximately equalled the amount of total external financing. The share of foreign direct investment was less than 5 per cent of the total, reflecting Korea's traditional reluctance to accept foreign investment, while about one-fifth of foreign borrowing went into reserve accumulation.

Net external financing averaged 8.5 per cent of Tunisia's GNP during the period under consideration; the corresponding ratio for total external financing was 11.8 per cent. Of the latter, foreign borrowing provided 57 per cent, foreign direct investment 23 per cent, and foreign aid (official capital) 11 per cent; changes in reserves were negligible.

Group II

Additional net external financing amounted to 60.1 per cent of the average value of exports and imports in Mexico, 83.5 per cent in Peru, and 51.6 per cent in Portugal in the years 1974-77, on average. The corresponding ratios were 3.4 per cent, 12.4 per cent, and 10.6 per cent if additional net external financing is related to the gross national product.

In the same period, the trend value of the resource gap was 0.9 per cent of GNP in Mexico, giving rise to an actual resource gap of 2.5 per cent of GNP. With large interest payments on foreign debt, which Mexico began to contract in substantial amounts in 1972, total external financing was much larger, averaging 6.3 per cent of GNP.

Recorded portfolio capital movements slightly exceeded Mexico's total financial requirements during the period under consideration. There were also negative errors and omissions, amounting to 37 per cent of the total, which largely reflected the clandestine outflow of capital during the Echevarria period. Finally, foreign direct investment provided 18 per cent of Mexico's total external financial requirements while there was little change in reserves.

In the years 1974-77, on average, the trend value of the resource gap was –1.9 per cent of the gross national product in Peru, resulting in actual net external financing of 10.5 per cent of GNP. With large foreign debts incurred in 1974 and in 1975, total external financing averaged 16.8 per cent of GNP during the period taken as a whole. Foreign borrowing provided three-fifths, direct foreign investment one-sixth, and the drawing down of reserves one-tenth of the total.

In Portugal, net external financial requirements averaged 7.3 per cent of GNP, representing a trend value of –3.3 per cent and additional net external financing of 10.6 per cent. The negative trend value is obtained by extrapolating Portugal's earlier export surplus that had given rise to a substantial accumulation of reserves. These reserves were used to provide two-fifths of Portugal's total financial requirements in 1974-77 which equalled 8.4 per cent of GNP.

Group III

In Colombia, the actual resource surplus averaged 2.5 per cent of GNP, in the 1974-77 period. With interest payments and dividends nearly matching this surplus, total external financing was approximately zero during this period. At the same time, Colombia accumulated reserves, financed largely by portfolio and direct investments.

In the Ivory Coast, the trend value of the resource gap amounted to 9.7 per cent of GNP, on average, in the period 1974-77, reflecting the fact that the continuation of past trends in exports and imports would have given rise to a growing deficit. This value, added to the actual resource surplus (1.8 per cent of GNP), yielded a saving in **additional** foreign borrowing of 11.5 per cent of GNP.

The Ivory Coast, however, incurred considerable interest and dividend charges on debt contracted in earlier years and on foreign direct investment, which had been the mainstay of its manufacturing sector. These charges raised total financing requirements to 5.0 per cent of GNP in the years 1974-77, on average. Portfolio capital more than provided for these requirements, while foreign direct investments were offset by the accumulation of reserves.

During the 1974-77 period, Malaysia had a surplus in both the actual and trend resource flows, which averaged, respectively, 6.9 and 1.6 per cent of GNP. Together, these flows gave rise to a saving in additional foreign borrowing of 5.3 per cent of GNP. Substantial dividend payments on foreign direct investments, however, equalled four-fifths of the actual resource surplus, resulting in total external financing of practically zero. At the same time, the large negative errors and omissions item much exceeded reported foreign borrowing in Malaysia, pointing to a net outflow of portfolio capital during the period under consideration, while foreign direct investment was nearly matched by the accumulation of reserves.

Export Promotion

Group I

Among the nine countries studied, Korea showed by far the best export performance in the 1974-77 period, on average, with increases in export market shares accounting for one-third of exports, inclusive of earnings from construction. Four-fifths of this gain originated in manufactured goods, where an upgrading and diversification of exports occurred. In particular, value added in the exports of textiles, clothing and shoes increased over time and new, skill-intensive export products assumed importance, including machinery and ships.

In percentage terms, however, the largest gains were made in traditional primary exports, with actual exports nearly double hypothetical exports, which were calculated on the assumption of unchanged market shares. Korea substantially increased its world market shares in fresh, chilled, and frozen fish and in crustaceans, and suffered only a small decline in the less important silk category.

Notwithstanding its poor natural resource endowment, Korea also made substantial gains in non-traditional primary products, raising these exports by over one-half. Finally, Korea's entire earnings from construction in the Middle East represented a gain, as its market share was practically zero before the oil crisis.

Increases in export market shares were much smaller in Brazil, accounting for 8 per cent of total exports in the 1974-77 period, on average. Brazil made gains in non-traditional primary and manufactured exports. In the first case, fruits, vegetables and vegetable oils (in particular, soybean oil, representing the domestic transformation of soybeans); in the second, non-electrical machinery, transport equipment, iron and steel, textiles, electrical machinery, footwear, and clothing – in this order – were responsible for the outcome.

Brazil experienced losses in the traditional primary export category, although a wide divergence was observed among individual commodities. Gains of 105 per cent were shown in the case of soybeans, 86 per cent for oilseeds, 57 per cent for iron ore, and 43 per cent for cocoa beans, with practically no change for castor oil. But cotton had losses of 76 per cent; meat, 69 per cent; sawnwood, 66 per cent; sugar, 32 per cent, and coffee, Brazil's largest export, 29 per cent.

Tunisia gained 9 per cent in its export market shares, the largest of which were in manufactured exports, increasing their market share by one-fourth. Substantial gains were also obtained in tourism and in remittances by emigrant workers, while small gains in fuels and in non-traditional primary exports were offset by small losses in traditional primary exports, on average.

Among traditional primary exports, Tunisia experienced gains of 6 per cent in olive oil, 25 per cent in almonds, and 59 per cent in lead ore. In turn, it incurred losses of 10 to 20 per cent in phosphates, wine, citrus products, and dates, and 65 to 70 per cent in iron ore and cereal products.

Group II

In the second group of countries, decreases in export market shares were responsible for a 17 per cent loss in Mexico's total exports in the years 1974-77, on average. The losses were largest in traditional primary exports, averaging about one-fifth. Among these products, Mexico experienced a gain in its world market share only in coffee, where actual exports exceeded hypothetical exports by one-fourth. Percentage losses for the other products were: sugar, 76 per cent; beef, 59 per cent; cattle, 43 per cent; crustaceans, 21 per cent; cotton, 8 per cent; and tomatoes, 2 per cent.

Moreover, Mexico suffered losses of about 15 per cent in its exports of non-traditional primary products and manufactured goods, 10 per cent in border transactions and 25 per cent in tourism. In contrast, actual exports exceeded hypothetical exports of fuels four-and-a-half times. This gain in fuel exports reduced the losses experienced in other commodity categories by 15 per cent.

Among the nine countries under consideration, Portugal suffered by far the largest losses in export market shares in the 1974-77 period, representing 38 per cent of its total exports. Notwithstanding gains obtained in the case of lumber (27 per cent) and cork (14 per cent), Portugal experienced a loss of 17 per cent in its traditional primary exports, taken together, as a result of losses incurred in the exports of tomatoes (49 per cent), canned and preserved fish (43 per cent), woodpulp (23 per cent), and wine (4 per cent). It also had a loss of 7 per cent in its market shares of non-traditional primary exports.

Portugal's losses were the largest in manufactured goods, where actual exports were only two-thirds of hypothetical exports, calculated on the assumption of unchanged market shares. Much of this represented a decline in manufactured exports to its former colonies, averaging $98 million between "1972" and 1974-77. The remaining loss of $22 million occurred in exports to the developed countries, where Portugal lost market shares to its competitors in Southern Europe and in the Far East. This result was obtained, notwithstanding a rise in market shares in the European Common Market, where Portugal received increased preferences because of losses in non-preferential markets, such as the United States, as well as in the member countries of the European Free Trade Association.

Portugal further experienced declines in tourism and in workers' remittances. Tourism in Portugal was adversely affected by unsettled conditions in the years following the revolution of April 1974, while policital uncertainty, the expectation of a large devaluation, and negative real interest rates discouraged the repatriation of earnings from abroad. With increased political stability, an exchange rate devaluation, and higher interest rates, improvements occurred in 1977 in regard to both foreign tourism and workers' remittances.

In contrast to Portugal and Mexico, Peru experienced a gain in export market shares that represented 14 per cent of its total exports in the years 1974-77, on average. Almost the entire gain was obtained in copper, Peru's leading export product, where actual exports were double the hypothetical exports. Gains were also obtained in other metals and sugar, but losses in cotton, wool, and fishery products.

Group III

Among the countries of the third group, Colombia experienced losses in exports of manufactured goods and fuels. In the first case, the elimination of export subsidies and the overvaluation of the exchange rate, and in the second, policy measures militating against new exploration were responsible for the outcome. These losses were only partially offset by gains in traditional and non-traditional primary exports.

Gains in non-traditional primary exports were observed in cut flowers, coffee essences, and rice. Among traditional exports, gains in cattle (119 per cent), bananas (101 per cent), cotton (19 per cent), and coffee (5 per cent) were not fully offset by losses in the exports of sugar (36 per cent) and beef (35 per cent).

Both the Ivory Coast and Malaysia obtained gains in export market shares in the years 1974-77, representing 25 per cent of total exports for the former, and 13 per cent for the latter. Apart from fuels in Malaysia, the two countries increased their export market shares in every commodity group.

In the Ivory Coast, gains in traditional primary exports were the largest in absolute, although not in relative, terms. They were concentrated in palm oil (56 per cent), coffee (45 per cent), lumber (31 per cent) and cocoa beans (30 per cent), followed by cotton (13 per cent) and cocoa paste (3 per cent), while the Ivory Coast experienced losses in the exports of bananas (11 per cent) and logs (3 per cent). At the same time, actual exports exceeded hypothetical exports, calculated on the assumption of unchanged market shares, by 83 per cent in the case of non-traditional primary exports and by 25 per cent in manufactured exports.

In Malaysia, gains of 38 per cent were experienced in non-traditional primary exports, 36 per cent in manufactured exports, and 10 per cent in traditional primary exports, with a loss of 11 per cent in fuels. All products showed a gain in the traditional primary group, with lumber (21 per cent) and logs (19 per cent) being followed by palmoil (16 per cent), tin (4 per cent), and rubber (3 per cent). At the same time, a variety of new exports appeared in the non-traditional primary and manufactured categories.

Import Substitution

Group I

Among the nine countries studied, Korea experienced the greatest effects of import substitution, which equalled 45 per cent of actual imports in the years 1974-77, on average. Expressed differently, actual imports were about one-third lower than hypothetical imports, calculated on the assumption of unchanged income elasticities of import demand.

Separate estimates of substitution were made for fuel and non-fuel imports. Korea's actual imports were less than hypothetical imports by one-fourth for fuels, and by one-third for non-fuels. The comparable figures were one-fifth and one-seventh in Brazil, averaging one-fifth for total imports.

In the same period, Tunisia experienced an increase in import shares amounting to 22 per cent of actual imports. This result was dominated by non-fuel imports; fuel imports were small during the period under consideration, averaging 6 per cent of the total, reflecting Tunisia's growing trade surplus in fuels.

Group II

Mexico, like Tunisia, experienced an increase in import shares, which raised its import bill by about one-fifth. Increased shares of non-fuel imports alone averaged 26 per cent of imports in the years 1974-77. In contrast, with the discovery of new deposits, actual fuel imports were two-thirds less than hypothetical fuel imports.

An increase in import shares was further observed in Peru, amounting to 14 per cent of import value in the years 1974-77, on average, with practically the same results shown for both fuel and non-fuel imports. In contrast, Portugal experienced slight import substitution, amounting to one-twentieth of actual imports. This outcome was the result of an increased share of fuels matched by a decreased share of non-fuel products imports (both 6 per cent).

Group III

In the third group, the Ivory Coast and Colombia experienced an increase in import shares, averaging 11 per cent and 6 per cent of total imports during the 1974-77 period, respectively. In contrast, Malaysia decreased its import share by 12 per cent.

In the Ivory Coast and in Colombia, increased import shares were shown in fuel as well as in non-fuel imports. In the Ivory Coast, actual imports exceeded hypothetical imports, by one-fourth and one-eigth in the two product groups, respectively.

Although actual fuel imports exceeded hypothetical imports two-and-a-half times in Colombia, these imports were relatively small in value, so that the outcome was dominated by non-fuel imports, where actual imports exceeded hypothetical imports by 6 per cent. Finally, in actual imports were 19 per cent below hypothetical imports for fuels in Malaysia. Malaysia import shares of fuels were reduced by one-fifth and of non-fuels by one-tenth.

Lowering Economic Growth Rates

Group I

Another form of policy response to adverse external shocks is to lower the rate of economic growth by the use of deflationary monetary and/or fiscal policies. However, in the countries of the first group, until 1977, average

GNP growth rates calculated on a "1972" basis were higher than in the 1963-73 period. In Brazil and in Tunisia, foreign borrowing contributed to this result, while in Korea foreign borrowing was followed by export expansion and import substitution that simultaneously raised GNP growth rates and improved the balance of payments.

Higher GNP growth rates, in turn, led to higher imports. This is shown by differences between trend and hypothetical imports, which have been calculated by combining income elasticities of import demand, estimated for the 1963-73 period, with GNP growth rates in that period and in the period under consideration, respectively. In the years 1974-77, on average, the excess of trend over hypothetical imports represented 19 per cent of actual imports in Korea and 7 per cent of actual imports in both Brazil and Tunisia.

Group II

In the second group, Mexico and Portugal experienced a decline in the rate of GNP growth, largely as a result of internal shocks. In Mexico, the disruptive effects of the policies followed under the Echeverria Administration, and in Portugal, the revolution of April 1974, contributed to this outcome. Lower GNP growth rates, in turn, led to decreases in imports of 4 per cent in Mexico and of 29 per cent in Portugal, in the years 1974-77, on average. In contrast, GNP growth rates in Peru were slightly higher than in 1963-73, raising imports by 2 per cent.

Group III

Among the countries of the third group, Malaysia utilised the increase in foreign exchange earnings, resulting from favourable external shocks, to increase its rate of economic growth, raising imports by 23 per cent in the years 1974-77, on average. Instead, growth rates declined in the Ivory Coast, lowering imports by 6 per cent while practically no change was shown in Colombia.

Comparative Analysis

In the following, we will contrast the balance-of-payments effects of the domestic policy measures – export promotion, import substitution, and lowering the rate of economic growth – with reliance on additional net external financing.

Considerable differences are observed among the countries of the first two groups. At one extreme, the favourable effects of internal policy measures exceeded the adverse balance-of-payments effects of external shocks by two-thirds in Korea. At the other extreme, domestic policies aggravated the adverse effects of external shocks in Mexico and in Tunisia, resulting in additional net external financing approximately double of the balance-of-payments impact of external shocks. In the same period, the balance-of-payments effects of domestic policies were nearly in balance in Peru and in Portugal, with additional net external financing exceeding the effects of adverse external shocks only slightly; it represented one-half of these effects in Brazil.

Considerable differences are also shown in the use of the various domestic policy measures. In the 1974-77 period, on the average, export promotion nearly matched, and import substitution surpassed, the adverse balance-of-payments effects of external shocks in Korea, while larger imports associated with higher GNP growth rates augmented these effects by one-half. In Brazil, import substitution predominated, offsetting one-half of the adverse balance-of-payments effects of external shocks. However, the export-raising effects of promotional measures were more than offset by the import-raising effects of higher GNP growth rates.

Tunisia experienced increased import shares in the 1974-77 period, which more than exceeded the adverse balance-of-payments effects of external shocks. And while increases in export market shares improved the balance of payments, they were nearly counterbalanced by the rise in imports associated with higher GNP growth rates.

In Mexico, increased import shares nearly doubled the adverse effects of external shocks in the 1974-77 period, on average. Mexico's balance-of-payments situation deteriorated further as a result of losses in export market shares, while import savings due to lower GNP growth rates were relatively small.

Peru experienced an increase in import shares, which added one-fifth to the adverse balance-of-payments effects of external shocks. Higher GNP growth rates also added slightly to imports, while the rise in export shares offset two-thirds of the total import increase. Finally, the decline in exports due to losses in market shares raised the adverse balance-of-payments effects of external shocks by four-fifths in Portugal, but these losses were nearly offset by savings in imports due to lower rates of GNP growth and, to a much lesser extent, import substitution.

Among the countries of the third group, domestic policies enhanced the favourable balance-of-payments effects of external shocks in Malaysia and the Ivory Coast. Malaysia experienced increases in export market shares and reduced import shares, which more than offset the rise in imports associated with the acceleration of GNP growth. Increases in market shares also led to a substantial rise in exports, while the lowering of the rate of GNP growth reduced import needs, in the Ivory Coast. These gains were only partially offset by the rise in import shares. In contrast, the negative balance-of-payments effects of domestic policies were twice as large as the effects of positive external shocks in Colombia, necessitating reliance on additional net external financing in the period 1974-77, on average.

TABLE III-1A - BALANCE OF PAYMENTS EFFECTS OF EXTERNAL SHOCKS

Balance-of-Payments Effects	Explanations	1974	1975	1976	1977	1974-75	1976-77	1974-77
		B R A Z I L						
I - External Shocks								
(1) Terms of Trade Effects	See text	3128	3292	2664	826	3210	1745	2478
(2) Export Volume Effects	in "1972"prices	179	530	314	770	355	542	449
(3) Together		3307	3822	2979	1596	3565	2288	2927
II - Policy Responses								
(4) Additional Net External Financing	See text	4569	2751	822	-2324	3660	- 751	1455
(5) Increase in Export Market Shares	in "1972"prices	104	779	344	526	442	435	439
(6) Import Substitution	idem	-742	733	2438	3608	- 5	3023	1509
(7) Import Effects of Lower GNP Growth Rates	idem	-624	-441	-625	- 214	- 532	- 419	-476
(8) Together		3307	3822	2979	1596	3565	2288	2927
III- Aggregate Values								
(9) Exports	in "1972"prices	4857	5509	5649	5776	5183	5714	5449
(10) Imports	idem	7946	7139	6583	6087	7543	6335	6939
(11) Average Trade	(9)+(10) : 2	6402	6324	6116	5932	6363	6025	6194
(12) Gross National Product	in "1972"prices	94570	99487	108143	112990	97029	110567	103798
		M E X I C O						
I - External Shocks								
(1) Terms of Trade Effects	See text	372	581	198	- 73	476	62	269
(2) Export Volume Effects	in "1972"prices	-103	504	369	771	201	570	386
(3) Together		269	1085	567	698	677	632	655
II - Policy Responses								
(4) Additional Net External Financing	See text	2032	2741	1765	926	2387	1345	1867
(5) Increase in Export Market Shares	in "1972"prices	-635	-701	-876	-441	-666	-659	-664
(6) Import Substitution	idem	-1135	-1032	-533	-79	-1084	-306	-695
(7) Import Effects of Lower GNP Growth Rates	idem	7	77	211	292	42	252	147
(8) Together		269	1085	567	698	677	632	655
III- Aggregate Values								
(9) Exports	in "1972"prices	3744	3450	3830	4328	3598	4079	3838
(10) Imports	idem	4351	4335	3870	3512	4343	3691	4017
(11) Average Trade	(9)+(10) : 2	4048	3893	3850	3920	3971	3885	3928
(12) Gross National Product	in "1972"prices	52549	54440	55148	57188	53495	56168	54832
		C O L O M B I A						
I - External Shocks								
(1) Terms of Trade Effects	See text	47	159	-139	-710	103	-425	-161
(2) Export Volume Effects	in "1972"prices	59	89	80	221	74	151	112
(3) Together		106	248	- 59	-489	177	-274	- 49
II - Policy Responses								
(4) Additional Net External Financing	See text	213	108	93	-227	161	- 67	47
(5) Increase in Export Market Shares	in "1972"prices	36	98	-128	-127	67	-128	- 30
(6) Import Substitution	idem	-133	46	- 23	-134	-44	- 79	- 61
(7) Import Effects of Lower GNP Growth Rates	idem	- 10	-4	- 1	- 1	- 7	- 1	- 4
(8) Together		106	248	- 59	-489	177	-274	- 49
III- Aggregate Values								
(9) Exports	in "1972"prices	996	1090	943	880	1043	912	978
(10) Imports	idem	1129	961	1047	1175	1045	1111	1078
(11) Average Trade	(9)+(10) : 2	1062	1026	995	1028	1044	1012	1028
(12) Gross National Effects	in "1972"prices	12277	12713	13281	13981	12495	13631	13082

Source : Appendix Table 1 and World Bank data bank.

AND OF POLICY RESPONSES TO THESE SHOCKS : ABSOLUTE VALUES ($ MILLION)

974	1975	1976	1977	1974-75	1976-77	1974-77	1974	1975	1976	1977	1974-75	1976-77	1974-77
			KOREA							TUNISIA			
638	1764	1119	242	1701	681	1191	- 140	49	149	159	- 45	154	55
108	497	212	662	303	437	370	43	94	106	163	68	135	101
746	2261	1331	904	2004	1118	1561	- 97	143	255	322	23	289	156
690	68	-1806	-3120	379	-2463	-1042	- 10	243	453	603	117	528	322
486	949	1836	2580	718	2208	1463	19	67	60	101	43	80	62
881	1613	2437	3109	1247	2773	2010	- 81	-116	-187	-311	-99	-249	-174
311	-369	-1136	-1665	-340	-1400	- 870	- 25	- 51	- 71	- 70	-38	- 70	- 54
746	2261	1331	904	2004	1118	1561	- 97	143	255	322	23	289	156
963	3414	5023	5823	3189	5423	4306	592	650	694	746	621	720	670
716	3832	4717	5687	3776	5204	4488	627	712	827	976	670	901	786
339	3623	4870	5755	3482	5313	4397	609	681	760	861	645	811	728
271	14357	16340	17987	13814	17164	15489	2260	2674	3126	3299	2467	3212	2840
			PERU							PORTUGAL			
299	955	875	805	627	840	734	408	520	796	885	464	840	652
260	325	415	278	32	346	189	99	540	428	745	320	587	453
39	1280	1290	1083	659	1186	923	507	1060	1224	1630	784	1427	1105
708	1483	1053	750	1096	902	999	961	827	1480	1665	894	1573	1233
290	184	301	360	- 53	331	139	-526	-758	-1198	-1037	-642	-1118	-879
327	-334	-35	-60	-330	- 48	-189	- 71	359	200	95	144	147	146
53	- 53	-28	32	- 53	2	- 26	143	632	742	907	388	825	606
38	1280	1291	1082	660	1187	923	507	1060	1224	1630	784	1427	1105
992	907	964	1196	950	1081	1015	2536	2138	2117	2311	2337	2213	2276
481	1529	1249	1262	1505	1255	1380	2678	2070	2467	2797	2374	2632	2503
236	1218	1106	1228	1227	1168	1197	2607	2104	2292	2554	2356	2422	2390
720	7982	8461	8139	7851	8300	8076	11727	11015	11570	12192	11371	11881	11626
			IVORY COAST							MALAYSIA			
125	0	-213	-558	- 63	-386	-225	-343	14	-814	-1270	-165	-1043	-604
62	127	105	199	95	152	124	88	342	243	435	215	339	277
63	127	-108	-359	32	-234	-101	-255	356	-571	- 835	50	- 704	-327
281	-17	-310	-503	-149	-407	-278	254	105	-996	- 988	179	- 992	-408
174	170	257	325	172	291	231	135	294	495	490	214	492	353
3	-89	- 83	-210	- 43	-147	- 95	-114	381	485	366	134	425	279
41	63	28	29	52	29	41	-530	-424	-555	- 703	-477	- 629	-553
-63	127	-108	-359	32	-234	-101	-255	356	-571	- 835	50	- 704	-327
838	812	967	992	825	980	903	2390	2440	2899	2876	2415	2887	2651
604	718	794	970	661	882	772	2610	2104	2232	2604	2357	2418	2388
721	765	881	981	743	931	837	2500	2272	2566	2740	2386	2653	2519
120	2268	2547	2718	2194	2633	2413	7237	7770	7770	8588	7327	8179	7753

TABLE III - 1B - BALANCE OF PAYMENTS EFFECTS OF EXTERNAL SHOCKS

Balance-of-Payments Effects	Explanations	1974	1975	1976	1977	1974-75	1976-77	1974-77
				B R A Z I L				
IV - External Shocks								
(13) Terms-of-Trade Effects/Average Trade	(1) : (11)	48.9	52.1	43.5	13.9	50.4	29.0	40.0
(14) Terms-of-Trade Effects/GNP	(1) : (12)	3.3	3.3	2.5	0.7	3.3	1.6	2.4
(15) Export Volume Effects/Exports	(2) : (9)	3.7	9.6	5.6	13.3	6.8	9.5	8.2
(16) Export Volume Effects/GNP	(2) : (12)	0.2	0.5	0.3	0.7	0.4	0.5	0.4
(17) External Shocks/GNP	(3) : (12)	3.5	3.8	2.8	1.4	3.7	2.1	2.8
V - Policy Responses								
(18) Additional Net External Financing/Average Trade	(4) : (11)	77.4	43.4	13.4	-39.2	57.5	-12.5	23.5
(19) Additional Net External Financing/GNP	(4) : (12)	4.8	2.8	0.8	- 2.1	3.8	- 0.7	1.4
(20) Increase in Export Shares/Exports	(5) : (9)	2.1	14.1	6.1	9.1	8.5	7.6	8.1
(21) Import Substitution/Imports	(6) : (10)	-9.3	10.3	37.0	59.3	0.0	47.7	21.7
(22) Import Effects of Lower GNP Growth Rate/Imports	(7) : (10)	-7.9	-6.2	-9.5	-3.5	-7.1	-6.6	-6.9
				M E X I C O				
IV - External Shocks								
(13) Terms-of-Trade Effects/Average Trade	(1) : (11)	9.1	14.9	5.1	-1.9	12.0	1.6	6.8
(14) Terms-of-Trade Effects/GNP	(1) : (12)	0.7	1.1	0.4	-0.6	0.9	0.1	0.5
(15) Export Volume Effects/Exports	(2) : (9)	-2.8	14.6	9.6	17.8	5.6	14.0	10.1
(16) Export Volume Effects/GNP	(2) : (12)	-0.2	0.9	0.7	1.3	0.4	1.0	0.7
(17) External Shocks/GNP	(3) : (12)	0.5	2.0	1.0	1.2	1.3	1.1	1.2
V - Policy Responses								
(18) Additional Net External Financing/Average Trade	(4) : (11)	50.2	70.4	45.8	23.6	60.1	34.6	47.5
(19) Additional Net External Financing/GNP	(4) : (11)	3.9	5.0	3.2	1.6	4.5	2.4	3.4
(20) Increase in Export Shares/Exports	(5) : (9)	-17.0	-20.3	-22.9	-10.2	-18.5	-16.2	-17.3
(21) Import Substitution/Imports	(6) : (10)	-26.1	-23.8	-13.8	- 2.2	-25.0	- 8.3	-17.3
(22) Import Effects of Lower GNP Growth Rate/Imports	(7) : (10)	0.2	1.8	5.5	8.3	1.0	6.8	3.7
				C O L O M B I A				
IV - External Shocks								
(13) Terms-of-Trade Effects/Average Trade	(1) : (11)	4.4	15.5	-14.0	-69.1	9.9	-42.0	-15.7
(14) Terms-of-Trade Effects/GNP	(1) : (12)	0.4	1.2	- 1.0	- 5.1	0.8	- 3.1	- 1.2
(15) Export Volume Effects/Exports	(2) : (9)	5.9	8.2	8.5	25.1	7.1	16.5	11.5
(16) Export Volume Effects/GNP	(2) : (12)	0.5	0.7	0.6	1.6	0.6	1.1	0.9
(17) External Shocks/GNP	(3) : (12)	0.9	2.0	-0.4	-3.5	1.4	- 2.0	- 0.4
V - Policy Responses								
(18) Additional Net External Financing/Average Trade	(4) : (11)	20.1	10.5	9.4	22.1	15.4	- 6.6	4.6
(19) Additional Net External Financing/ GNP	(4) : (11)	1.7	0.9	0.7	1.6	1.3	- 0.5	0.4
(20) Increase in Export Shares/Exports	(5) : (9)	3.6	9.0	-13.5	-14.5	6.4	-14.0	-3.1
(21) Import Substitution/Imports	(6) : (10)	-11.8	4.8	- 2.2	-11.4	-4.2	- 7.1	-5.8
(22) Import Effects of Lower GNP Growth Rate/Imports	(7) : (10)	- 0.9	-0.4	- 0.1	- 1.0	-0.7	- 0.1	-0.4

AND OF POLICY RESPONSES TO THESE SHOCKS : RATIOS (per cent)

1974	1975	1976	1977	1974-75	1976-77	1974-77	1974	1975	1976	1977	1974-75	1976-77	1974-77
KOREA							TUNISIA						
49.1	48.7	23.0	4.2	48.9	12.8	27.1	-23.0	7.2	19.6	18.5	-7.0	18.9	7.5
12.3	12.3	6.8	1.3	12.3	4.0	7.7	- 6.2	1.8	4.8	4.8	-1.8	4.8	1.9
3.6	14.6	4.2	11.4	9.5	8.1	8.6	7.3	14.5	15.3	21.9	11.1	18.7	15.2
0.8	3.5	1.3	3.7	2.2	2.5	2.4	1.9	3.5	3.4	4.9	2.8	4.2	3.6
13.2	15.7	8.1	5.0	14.5	6.5	10.1	- 4.3	5.4	8.1	9.8	0.9	9.0	5.5
20.7	1.9	-37.1	-54.2	10.9	-46.4	-23.7	1.7	35.7	59.5	70.0	18.1	65.1	44.3
5.2	0.5	-11.1	-17.3	2.7	-14.3	- 6.7	- 0.5	9.1	14.5	18.3	4.7	16.4	11.3
16.4	27.8	36.6	44.3	22.5	40.7	33.2	3.2	10.3	8.6	13.5	6.9	11.2	9.2
23.7	42.1	51.7	54.7	33.0	53.3	44.8	-12.9	-16.3	-22.7	-31.9	-14.7	-27.7	-22.1
-8.4	- 9.6	-24.1	-29.3	- 9.0	-26.9	-19.4	- 4.0	- 7.2	- 8.6	- 7.2	- 5.7	- 7.8	- 6.9
PERU							PORTUGAL						
24.2	78.4	79.1	65.5	51.1	71.9	61.3	15.7	24.7	34.7	34.7	19.4	34.7	27.3
3.9	12.0	10.3	9.9	8.0	10.1	9.1	3.5	4.7	6.9	7.3	4.1	7.1	5.6
-26.2	35.8	43.0	23.2	3.4	32.0	18.6	3.9	25.3	20.2	32.2	13.7	26.5	19.9
- 3.4	4.1	4.9	3.4	0.4	4.2	2.3	0.8	4.9	3.7	6.1	2.8	4.9	3.9
0.5	16.0	15.2	13.3	8.4	14.3	11.4	4.3	9.6	10.6	13.4	6.9	12.0	9.5
57.3	121.8	95.2	61.1	89.3	77.2	83.5	36.9	39.3	64.6	65.2	37.9	64.9	151.6
9.2	18.6	12.4	9.2	14.0	10.9	12.4	8.2	7.5	12.8	13.7	7.9	13.2	10.6
-29.2	20.3	31.2	30.1	- 3.4	30.6	13.7	-20.7	-35.5	-56.6	-44.9	-27.5	-50.5	-38.6
-22.1	-21.8	-2.8	-4.8	-21.9	-3.8	-13.7	- 2.5	17.3	8.1	3.4	6.1	5.6	5.8
- 3.6	- 3.5	-2.2	2.5	- 3.5	0.2	- 1.9	5.0	30.5	30.1	32.4	16.3	31.3	24.2
IVORYCOAST							MALAYSIA						
-17.3	0.0	-24.2	-56.9	- 8.5	-41.5	-26.9	-13.7	0.6	-31.5	-46.4	- 6.9	-39.3	-24.0
- 5.9	0.0	- 8.4	-20.5	- 2.9	-14.7	- 9.3	- 4.7	0.2	-10.5	-14.8	- 2.3	-12.8	- 7.8
7.4	15.6	13.2	20.1	11.5	16.7	14.1	3.7	14.1	8.4	15.1	8.9	11.7	10.4
2.9	5.6	4.1	7.3	4.3	5.8	5.1	1.2	4.6	3.1	5.1	2.9	4.1	3.6
- 3.0	5.6	- 4.2	-13.2	1.5	- 8.9	- 4.2	- 3.5	4.8	- 7.4	- 9.7	0.6	- 8.7	- 4.2
-39.0	-2.2	-35.2	-51.2	-20.1	-43.7	-33.2	10.2	4.6	-36.6	-36.1	7.5	-37.4	-16.2
-13.3	-0.7	-12.2	-18.5	- 6.8	-15.5	-11.5	3.5	1.4	-12.8	-11.5	2.4	-12.1	- 5.3
20.8	20.9	26.6	32.8	20.9	29.7	25.3	5.6	12.0	17.1	17.1	8.9	17.0	13.3
0.5	-12.4	-10.5	-21.6	- 6.0	-16.1	-11.3	- 4.4	18.1	21.7	14.1	5.7	17.6	11.7
6.8	8.8	3.5	3.0	7.8	3.3	5.6	-20.3	-20.2	-24.6	-27.0	-20.2	-26.0	-23.2

TABLE III-2

FINANCING THE EXTERNAL RESOURCE GAP ($ MILLION IN CURRENT PRICES)

BRAZIL	1971	1972	1973	"1972"	1974	1975	1976	1977	1978
Interest Receipts	43	131	327	167	718	364	282	358	640
Interest Payments	-374	-544	-908	-609	-1448	-1861	-2091	-2460	-3334
Dividends	-412	-310	-530	-417	-554	-532	-790	-1330	-1538
Other Factor Payments	8	8	10	9	-1	-75	-120	-33	-44
Official Transfers	20	23	16	20	-2	-10	-4	5	3
Direct Investment	536	570	1341	816	1268	1090	1212	1678	1880
Portfolio Capital	1595	3115	4109	2493	5371	4956	6988	4540	9486
Errors and Omissions	-9	438	355	261	-64	-35	1024	-614	298
Changes in Reserves	-483	-2431	-2307	-1740	989	1016	-2683	-495	-4646
Net External Financing	924	1000	1072	1000	6277	4913	3818	1649	2742
Total External Financing	1710	1854	2510	2026	8279	7306	6699	5439	7614
Amortization	-850	-1202	-1673	-1242	-1920	-2172	-2992	-4060	-5170

KOREA	1971	1972	1973	"1972"	1974	1975	1976	1977	1978
Interest Receipts	23	21	41	28	82	45	71	144	282
Interest Payments	-109	-150	-204	-154	-293	-403	-485	-725	-968
Dividends	-3	-9	-10	-7	-30	-24	-37	-61	-50
Other Factor Payments	24	22	29	25	28	32	50	108	103
Official Transfers	66	51	35	51	68	69	155	51	39
Direct Investment	663	572	93	618	105	53	75	73	61
Portfolio Capital			587		796	1805	1653	1261	934
Errors and Omissions	230	316	271	272	203	226	303	519	447
Changes in Reserves	172	-182	-390	-133	1094	151	-1174	-1315	402
Net External Financing	1066	581	452	700	2053	1954	611	55	1250
Total External Financing	1178	740	666	862	2376	2381	1133	841	2268
Amortization	-135	-202	-261	-199	-338	-284	-407	-536	-825

TUNISIA	1971	1972	1973	"1972"	1974	1975	1976	1977	1978
Interest Receipts	5	8	18	10	36	36	23	14	21
Interest Payments	-21	-22	-37	-26	-38	-66	-70	-84	-125
Dividends	-3	-24	-31	-19	-33	-30	-28	-26	-31
Other Factor Payments	na	na	na	na	na	na	na	na	na
Official Transfers	25	32	38	32	21	38	48	44	33
Direct Investment	23	32	57	37	49	58	110	93	91
Portfolio Capital	63	39	75	59	23	113	240	385	510
Errors and Omissions	-2	3	7	3	-13	-5	22	-3	-6
Changes in Reserves	-94	-74	-78	-83	-88	17	16	59	30
Net External Financing	-4	-6	49	13	-43	161	361	482	463
Total External Financing	20	40	117	58	28	257	459	592	619
Amortization	-46	-66	-79	-64	-71	-88	-88	-96	-140

MEXICO	1971	1972	1973	"1972"	1974	1975	1976	1977	1978
Interest Receipts	65	80	97	81	153	117	124	168	245
Interest Payments	-309	-345	-513	-389	-806	-1094	-1675	-1978	-2550
Dividends	-359	-435	-581	-458	-794	-840	-666	-400	-480
Other Factor Payments	133	149	157	146	182	186	253	260	279
Official Transfers	7	10	8	8	22	27	27	16	18
Direct Investment	307	301	457	355	678	610	628	556	532
Portfolio Capital	629	154	1524	769	3122	4872	5233	1616	2956
Errors and Omissions	34	651	-411	91	-845	-1249	-3046	53	-557
Changes in Reserves	-134	-190	-154	-159	-79	-178	595	-375	-428
Net External Financing	373	375	584	444	1633	2451	1473	-84	15
Total External Financing	1041	1155	1678	1291	3233	4385	3814	2294	3045
Amortization	-479	-531	-877	-629	-592	-835	-1258	-2420	-4490

PERU	1971	1972	1973	"1972"	1974	1975	1976	1977	1978
Interest Receipts	19	13	25	19	38	34	10	13	15
Interest Payments	-94	-87	-108	-97	-168	-261	-337	-381	-507
Dividends	-50	-47	-80	-59	-42	-15	-44	-55	-84
Other Factor Payments	-14	-13	-14	-14	-13	-17	-13	-25	-23
Official Transfers	35	33	42	37	26	33	55	54	54
Direct Investment	-58	24	70	15	58	316	170	54	25
Portfolio Capital	-88	104	325	114	1136	920	1038	1046	138
Errors and Omissions	40	-64	-20	-15	-25	-175	-329	-89	58
Changes in Reserves	48	-9	-92	-18	-397	495	314	-65	-19
Net External Financing	-162	-46	148	-20	613	1330	880	552	-343
Total External Financing	-18	88	336	135	823	1606	1261	968	934
Amortization	-225	-225	-381	-277	-397	-433	-451	-496	-944

PORTUGAL	1971	1972	1973	"1972"	1974	1975	1976	1977	1978
Interest Receipts	36	79	136	84	179	90	30	43	63
Interest Payments	-25	-33	-31	-30	-41	-103	-136	-208	-387
Dividends	-24	-29	-31	-28	-34	-13	-25	-13	-5
Other Factor Payments	-	-	-	-	-	-	-	-	-
Official Transfers	-	-	-	-	-	-	-	-	-
Direct Investment	49	66	51	55	69	106	46	57	56
Portfolio Capital	35	-13	-176	-105	-201	-199	-17	-14	702
Errors and Omissions	108	73	111	97	-30	-112	141	472	27
Changes in Reserves	-340	-320	-327	-329	590	1046	1068	961	-41
Net External Financing	-158	-333	-255	-250	958	755	1107	1298	497
Total External Financing	-37	-125	-99	-52	1120	1270	1698	2072	1654
Amortization	-96	-175	-233	-168	-121	-412	-455	-566	-770

COLOMBIA	1971	1972	1973	"1972"	1974	1975	1976	1977	1978
Interest Receipts	9	18	24	17	65	56	65	65	123
Interest Payments	-114	-135	-168	-139	-201	-250	-269	-252	-269
Dividends	-71	-70	-70	-70	-55	-68	-109	-86	-114
Other Factor Payments	-32	-33	-25	-30	-23	-18	-17	-2	-3
Official Transfers	31	24	23	26	32	17	13	6	6
Direct Investment	43	18	24	28	4	40	25	64	75
Portfolio Capital	303	228	123	218	231	142	171	-91	149
Errors and Omissions	90	103	69	87	-17	10	211	159	138
Changes in Reserves	1	-178	-161	-113	95	-112	-633	-586	-528
Net External Financing	260	-25	-161	25	168	-183	-543	-723	-423
Total External Financing	445	180	77	234	424	135	-165	-385	-40
Amortization	-171	-180	-190	-180	-264	-221	-217	-232	-282

IVORY COAST	1971	1972	1973	"1972"	1974	1975	1976	1977	1978
Interest Receipts	8	7	8	8	16	25	10	16	24
Interest Payments	-19	-24	-33	-25	-42	-58	-79	-93	-110
Dividends	-39	-41	-80	-53	-73	-104	-90	-117	-171
Other Factor Payments	-42	-45	-73	-54	-61	-133	-156	-239	-297
Official Transfers	33	33	48	38	41	36	20	35	13
Direct Investment	16	19	51	29	32	81	37	2	27
Portfolio Capital	65	18	151	78	136	125	235	380	825
Errors and Omissions	9	0	7	5	-21	14	10	-24	0
Changes in Reserves	16	81	10	36	-88	164	-33	-182	-133
Net External Financing	47	48	89	62	-60	150	-46	-222	178
Total External Financing	105	113	202	140	56	312	123	-12	459
Amortization	-28	-37	-43	-36	-73	-74	-134	-193	-244

MALAYSIA	1971	1972	1973	"1972"	1974	1975	1976	1977	1978
Interest Receipts	87	74	105	88	142	126	130	181	268
Interest Payments	-33	-43	-69	-48	-90	-93	-109	-168	-263
Dividends	-173	-165	-305	-214	-467	-336	-410	-531	-700
Other Factor Payments	-1	-1	-1	-1	1	1	23	35	87
Official Transfers	17	7	14	13	8	16	9	8	14
Direct Investment	100	114	172	129	571	359	300	481	523
Portfolio Capital	185	187	166	180	129	347	153	-277	19
Errors and Omissions	-112	-26	-219	-119	-20	-324	-388	-444	-498
Changes in Reserves	-215	-41	-227	-161	-271	89	-828	-486	-468
Net External Financing	-144	106	-364	-133	3	185	-1120	-1201	-1018
Total External Financing	62	314	10	129	560	614	-701	-502	-55
Amortization	-12	-18	-22	-17	-46	-45	-47	-81	-100

Source: International Monetary Fund, Balance-of-Payments Yearbook

TABLE III-3

NOMINAL AND REAL INTEREST RATES, THE MONEY SUPPLY AND THE GOVERNMENT BUDGET (AS A PERCENT OF GNP)

BRAZIL

	1971	1972	1973	"1972"	1974	1975	1976	1977	1978
Nominal Interest Rate	20.0	20.0	18.0	19.3	18.0	18.0	28.0	30.0	33.0
Real Interest Rate	0.0	1.2	1.1	0.8	-8.6	-7.3	-10.7	-8.7	-3.3
Government Revenue	9.8	10.5	10.7	10.3	10.8	9.6	10.8	10.6	10.4
Government Expenditure	10.1	10.6	10.6	10.4	10.2	9.6	10.8	10.6	10.3
Government Budget Surplus (Deficit)	-0.2	-0.1	0.1	-0.1	0.6	0.6	0.0	0.0	0.1

KOREA

	1971	1972	1973	"1972"	1974	1975	1976	1977	1978
Nominal Interest Rate	16.0	11.0	11.0	12.7	11.0	14.0	14.0	14.0	15.0
Real Interest Rate	-6.9	-2.4	3.8	2.7	-21.9	-9.9	1.7	4.6	3.0
Government Revenue	17.2	15.6	15.4	16.1	16.0	17.7	20.7	19.7	20.3
Government Expenditure	17.8	20.1	16.6	18.2	17.8	19.4	20.3	19.4	19.8
Government Budget Surplus (Deficit)	-0.6	-4.5	1.2	-2.1	-1.8	-1.7	0.4	0.3	0.5

TUNISIA

	1971	1972	1973	"1972"	1974	1975	1976	1977	1978
Nominal Interest Rate	5.0	5.0	5.0	5.0	5.0	5.0	5.0	5.8	5.8
Real Interest Rate	-2.1	3.4	-0.3	0.3	-13.3	-4.1	3.8	0.9	2.5
Government Revenue	na	na	25.0	na	26.2	28.6	28.7	30.4	32.6
Government Expenditure	na	na	26.0	na	26.8	29.8	31.5	35.3	35.3
Government Budget Surplus (Deficit)	na	na	-1.0	na	-0.6	-1.2	-2.8	-4.9	-2.7

MEXICO

	1971	1972	1973	"1972"	1974	1975	1976	1977	1978
Nominal Interest Rate	4.5	4.5	4.5	4.5	4.5	4.5	4.5	4.5	4.5
Real Interest Rate	0.6	1.7	-8.8	-2.2	-14.7	-5.4	-14.6	-26.0	-9.7
Government Revenue	8.5	9.7	10.9	9.7	11.4	13.2	13.1	11.6	19.4
Government Expenditure	9.3	11.6	14.1	11.7	15.0	16.3	16.5	14.9	24.1
Government Budget Surplus (Deficit)	-0.8	-1.9	-3.2	-2.0	-3.6	-3.1	-3.4	-3.3	-4.7

PERU

	1971	1972	1973	"1972"	1974	1975	1976	1977	1978
Nominal Interest Rate	9.5	9.5	9.5	9.5	9.5	9.5	12.5	14.5	28.5
Real Interest Rate	2.4	2.2	0.0	1.5	-6.3	-11.4	-15.7	-17.1	-18.6
Government Revenue	15.8	15.6	15.0	15.5	15.4	15.9	14.7	15.0	16.3
Government Expenditure	18.9	19.3	19.0	19.2	18.6	21.5	21.1	22.6	21.5
Government Budget Surplus (Deficit)	-3.1	-3.7	-4.0	-3.6	-3.2	-5.6	-6.4	-7.6	-5.2

PORTUGAL

	1971	1972	1973	"1972"	1974	1975	1976	1977	1978
Nominal Interest Rate	3.8	4.0	5.0	4.3	7.5	6.5	6.5	13.0	18.0
Real Interest Rate	0.2	1.0	-5.7	-1.5	-16.7	-5.2	-10.5	-12.7	-10.0
Government Revenue	26.1	25.8	25.1	25.6	23.0	27.4	30.2	29.2	29.5
Government Expenditure	23.8	25.1	23.6	24.2	24.7	32.9	37.2	36.5	38.4
Government Budget Surplus (Deficit)	2.2	0.6	1.4	1.4	-2.2	-5.4	-7.0	-7.3	-8.9

COLOMBIA

	1971	1972	1973	"1972"	1974	1975	1976	1977	1978
Nominal Interest Rate	14.0	14.0	14.0	14.0	16.0	16.0	20.0	20.0	20.0
Real Interest Rate	2.2	-3.7	-10.9	-4.1	-14.8	-7.5	-2.1	-5.3	-1.9
Government Revenue	9.7	8.9	8.4	9.1	8.1	9.5	9.3	9.0	9.5
Government Expenditure	10.5	10.9	9.4	10.3	9.0	9.8	8.5	8.1	8.8
Government Budget Surplus (Deficit)	-0.8	-2.0	-1.0	-1.3	-0.9	-0.3	0.9	0.8	0.7

IVORY COAST

	1971	1972	1973	"1972"	1974	1975	1976	1977	1978
Nominal Interest Rate	3.5	3.5	5.5	4.2	5.5	8.0	8.0	8.0	8.0
Real Interest Rate	5.2	3.2	-5.1	1.1	-10.0	-3.1	-3.7	-15.2	-4.4
Government Revenue	21.2	22.3	21.4	21.6	20.3	23.7	27.7	30.3	32.0
Government Expenditure	16.9	17.8	17.1	17.3	16.8	25.8	28.6	27.7	32.1
Government Budget Surplus (Deficit)	4.4	4.5	4.3	4.4	3.5	-2.1	-1.0	2.6	-0.1

MALAYSIA

	1971	1972	1973	"1972"	1974	1975	1976	1977	1978
Nominal Interest Rate	na	na	na	na	na	na	na	na	na
Real Interest Rate	na	na	na	na	na	na	na	na	na
Government Revenue	19.5	21.6	19.1	20.1	22.0	23.7	22.8	25.1	25.3
Government Expenditure	25.0	30.0	22.8	25.9	24.8	28.5	27.4	30.4	30.4
Government Budget Surplus (Deficit)	-5.5	-8.4	-3.7	-5.8	-2.8	-4.8	-4.6	-5.3	-5.1

Source: International Monetary Fund, *International Financial Statistics*

Note : Data on government budget surplus (deficit) do not include grants and lending loss.

TABLE III-4

NOMINAL AND REAL EXCHANGE RATES

	1971	1972	1973	"1972"	1974	1975	1976	1977	1978	1971	1972	1973	"1972"	1974	1975	1976	1977	1978	1971	1972	1973	"1972"	1974	1975	1976	1977	1978
	BRAZIL									KOREA									TUNISIA								
Exchange Rate, National Currency/U.S. Dollar	5.288	5.934	6.126	5.783	6.790	8.129	10.675	14.144	18.070	350.1	394.0	398.5	380.9	406.0	484.0	484.0	484.0	484.0	.5213	.4772	.4200	.4728	.4365	.4023	.4288	.4290	.4160
Index of Exchange Rate	86.3	96.9	100.0	94.4	110.8	132.7	174.3	230.9	295.0	87.9	98.9	100.0	95.6	101.9	121.5	121.5	121.5	121.5	124.1	113.6	100.0	112.6	104.0	95.8	102.2	102.2	99.1
Index of Relative Prices vis-à-vis:																											
United States	85.2	96.8	100.0	94.0	108.8	126.5	173.5	232.7	297.4	97.1	105.8	100.0	101.0	119.5	138.5	148.5	152.5	157.9	110.4	107.4	100.0	105.9	101.9	102.2	98.8	97.6	93.5
Principal Trading Partners	91.1	100.6	100.0	97.2	106.6	126.3	173.1	229.6	288.0	105.2	111.4	100.0	105.5	119.2	141.2	152.0	152.9	148.6	na	115.3	100.0	na	99.5	101.0	103.4	102.4	92.8
Index of Real Exchange Rates vis-à-vis:																											
United States $	101.3	100.1	100.0	100.5	101.8	104.9	100.5	99.2	99.2	90.5	93.5	100.0	94.7	85.3	87.7	81.8	79.7	76.5	112.4	105.8	100.0	106.1	102.0	93.8	103.4	104.7	106.0
Currencies of Major Trading Partners	94.7	96.3	100.0	97.0	103.9	105.1	100.7	100.6	102.4	83.6	88.8	100.0	90.6	85.5	86.0	79.9	79.5	81.8	na	98.5	100.0	na	104.5	94.9	98.8	99.7	106.7

	1971	1972	1973	"1972"	1974	1975	1976	1977	1978	1971	1972	1973	"1972"	1974	1975	1976	1977	1978	1971	1972	1973	"1972"	1974	1975	1976	1977	1978
	MEXICO									PERU									PORTUGAL								
Exchange Rate, National Currency/U.S. Dollar	12.50	12.50	12.50	12.50	12.50	12.50	15.43	22.57	22.77	38.70	38.70	38.70	38.70	38.70	40.80	57.43	86.96	158.85	28.32	27.01	24.67	26.67	25.41	25.55	30.22	38.28	43.94
Index of Exchange Rate	100.0	100.0	100.0	100.0	100.0	100.0	123.4	180.6	182.1	100.0	100.0	100.0	100.0	100.0	105.4	148.4	224.7	410.5	114.8	109.5	100.0	108.0	103.0	103.6	122.5	155.1	178.1
Index of Relative Prices vis-à-vis:																											
United States	99.2	97.6	100.0	99.0	103.1	104.2	121.9	162.0	174.2	93.6	97.0	100.0	96.9	105.4	119.3	147.4	188.1	272.3	97.3	100.8	100.0	99.4	105.8	103.9	120.4	146.3	190.4
Principal Trading Partners	103.1	99.7	100.0	100.9	103.0	104.7	122.6	161.7	170.8	96.5	98.5	100.0	98.3	102.7	114.9	144.0	171.8	241.3	na	na	100.0	na	105.6	102.2	124.0	145.9	177.4
Index of Real Exchange Rates vis-à-vis:																											
United States $	100.8	102.5	100.0	101.0	97.0	96.0	101.2	111.5	104.5	106.8	103.1	100.0	103.3	94.9	88.3	100.7	119.5	150.8	118.0	108.6	100.0	108.9	97.4	99.7	101.7	106.0	93.5
Currencies of Major Trading Partners	97.0	100.3	100.0	99.1	97.1	95.5	100.6	111.7	106.6	103.6	101.5	100.0	101.6	97.4	91.7	103.1	130.8	170.1	na	na	100.0	na	97.4	101.4	98.8	106.3	100.4

	1971	1972	1973	"1972"	1974	1975	1976	1977	1978	1971	1972	1973	"1972"	1974	1975	1976	1977	1978	1971	1972	1973	"1972"	1974	1975	1976	1977	1978
	COLOMBIA									IVORY COAST									MALAYSIA								
Exchange Rate, National Currency/U.S. Dollar	20.08	22.02	23.81	21.97	27.11	31.20	34.98	37.00	39.32	277.0	252.2	222.7	250.6	240.5	214.3	239.0	245.7	225.6	3.020	2.805	2.443	2.756	2.407	2.402	2.542	2.461	2.316
Index of Exchange Rate	84.3	92.5	100.0	92.3	113.9	131.0	146.9	155.4	165.1	124.4	113.3	100.0	112.6	108.0	96.2	107.3	110.3	101.3	123.6	114.8	100.0	112.8	98.5	98.3	104.1	100.8	94.8
Index of Relative Prices vis-à-vis:																											
United States	78.1	88.4	100.0	88.8	114.5	131.4	154.4	184.4	201.1	102.6	99.4	100.0	100.7	106.6	102.8	117.3	145.7	138.2	96.4	96.2	100.0	97.5	105.9	101.3	98.3	96.7	94.3
Principal Trading Partners										121.9	109.0	100.0	110.3	106.3	103.4	124.9	154.2	138.4	122.0	112.5	100.0	111.5	101.7	94.8	91.2	85.7	78.1
Index of Real Exchange Rates vis-à-vis:																											
United States $	107.9	104.6	100.0	104.1	99.5	99.7	95.1	84.3	82.1	121.2	114.0	100.0	111.7	101.3	93.6	91.5	75.7	73.3	128.2	119.3	100.0	115.8	93.0	97.0	105.9	104.2	100.5
Currencies of Major Trading Partners										102.1	113.9	100.0	105.3	101.6	93.0	85.9	71.5	73.2	101.3	102.0	100.0	101.1	96.9	103.7	114.1	117.6	121.4

Source: International Monetary Fund, International Financial Statistics and International Trade Statistics.

TABLE III-5

INTEREST, DEBT SERVICE, AND DEBT SERVICE DATA ($ MILLION IN ANNUAL PRICES)

BRAZIL	1971	1972	1973	"1972"	1974	1975	1976	1977	1978
Gross Debt Service	1224	1746	2581	1851	3368	4033	5083	6520	8504
Net Debt Service	1181	1615	2254	1684	2650	3669	4801	6162	7764
Merchandise Exports	2904	3991	6199	4365	7951	8670	10128	12120	12659
Gross Debt Service Ratio	42.1	43.7	41.6	42.4	42.4	46.5	50.2	53.8	67.2
Net Debt Service Ratio	40.7	40.5	36.4	38.6	33.3	42.3	47.4	50.8	67.4
Gross External Debt	6622	9521	12572	9572	17166	21171	25985	32037	43510
Net Reserves	1723	4183	6416	4107	5269	4041	6544	7256	11895
Net External Debt	4899	5338	6156	5465	11897	17130	19441	24781	31615
Gross National Product	64340	74871	90227	76479	108664	125212	143198	158556	180024
Gross External Debt Ratio	10.3	12.7	13.9	12.5	16.0	16.9	18.1	20.2	24.2
Net External Debt Ratio	7.6	7.1	6.8	7.1	10.9	13.7	13.6	15.6	17.6

KOREA	1971	1972	1973	"1972"	1974	1975	1976	1977	1978
Gross Debt Service	244	352	465	353	631	687	892	1261	1793
Net Debt Service	221	331	424	325	549	642	821	1117	1511
Merchandise Exports	1068	1624	3225	1972	4460	5081	7715	10041	12711
Gross Debt Service Ratio	22.8	21.7	14.4	17.9	14.1	13.5	11.6	12.6	14.1
Net Debt Service Ratio	20.7	20.4	13.1	16.5	12.3	12.6	10.6	11.1	11.9
Gross External Debt			3556		4693	6047	7370	8622	11992
Net Reserves			889		282	786	1975	2973	2794
Net External Debt			2667		4411	5261	5395	5649	9198
Gross National Product			20159		23775	27894	33516	40070	47996
Gross External Debt Ratio			17.6		19.7	21.7	22.0	21.5	25.0
Net External Debt Ratio			13.2		18.6	18.9	16.1	14.1	19.2

TUNISIA	1971	1972	1973	"1972"	1974	1975	1976	1977	1978
Gross Debt Service	61	88	116	90	109	154	158	180	265
Net Debt Service	62	80	98	80	73	118	135	166	246
Merchandise Exports	214	313	416	314	872	799	779	772	894
Gross Debt Service Ratio	31.3	28.1	27.9	28.6	12.5	19.3	20.3	23.3	29.6
Net Debt Service Ratio	29.0	25.6	23.6	25.5	8.4	14.8	17.3	21.5	27.5
Gross External Debt			905		1033	1143	1292	1924	2600
Net Reserves			307		419	386	371	358	450
Net External Debt			598		614	757	921	1566	2150
Gross National Product			2799		3371	4082	4551	5052	5954
Gross External Debt Ratio			32.3		30.6	28.0	28.4	38.1	43.7
Net External Debt Ratio			21.4		18.2	18.5	20.2	31.0	36.1

MEXICO	1971	1972	1973	"1972"	1974	1975	1976	1977	1978
Gross Debt Service	788	876	1390	1018	1398	1929	2933	4398	7040
Net Debt Service	723	796	1293	937	1245	1812	2809	4230	6795
Merchandise Exports	1363	1665	2071	1700	2850	2861	3316	4418	6217
Gross Debt Service Ratio	57.8	52.6	67.1	59.9	49.1	67.4	88.4	99.5	113.2
Net Debt Service Ratio	53.0	47.8	62.4	55.1	43.7	63.3	84.7	95.7	109.3
Gross External Debt			8310		12389	17263	22000	26785	32622
Net Reserves			1355		1393	1539	1027	1419	1947
Net External Debt			6955		10996	15724	20973	25366	30675
Gross National Product			52391		60478	68624	73159	80402	91914
Gross External Debt Ratio			15.9		20.5	25.2	30.1	33.3	35.5
Net External Debt Ratio			13.3		18.2	22.9	28.7	31.5	33.3

PERU	1971	1972	1973	"1972"	1974	1975	1976	1977	1978
Gross Debt Service	319	312	489	373	565	694	788	877	1451
Net Debt Service	300	299	464	354	527	660	778	864	1436
Merchandise Exports	890	945	1112	982	1503	1291	1360	1726	1933
Gross Debt Service Ratio	35.8	33.0	44.0	38.0	37.5	53.8	57.9	50.8	75.1
Net Debt Service Ratio	33.7	31.6	41.7	36.0	35.0	51.0	57.2	50.1	74.3
Gross External Debt			2682		3442	4380	5100	6140	6710
Net Reserves			552		968	468	148	194	99
Net External Debt			2130		2474	3912	4952	5946	6611
Gross National Product			7562		8883	10067	10656	10857	11442
Gross External Debt Ratio			35.5		38.7	43.5	47.9	56.6	58.6
Net External Debt Ratio			28.0		27.9	38.9	46.5	54.8	57.8

PORTUGAL	1971	1972	1973	"1972"	1974	1975	1976	1977	1978
Gross Debt Service	121	208	264	198	162	515	591	774	1157
Net Debt Service	85	129	128	114	-17	425	561	731	1058
Merchandise Exports	2008	2602	3499	2703	3907	3331	3112	3567	4643
Gross Debt Service Ratio	6.0	8.0	7.5	7.3	4.1	15.5	19.0	21.7	24.9
Net Debt Service Ratio	4.2	5.0	3.7	4.2	0.4	12.8	18.0	20.5	22.8
Gross External Debt			1296		1642	1720	2892	4426	5420
Net Reserves			2839		2354	1534	1100	1094	1616
Net External Debt			-1543		-712	186	1792	3332	3804
Gross National Product			11494		13449	14711	15339	16078	17465
Gross External Debt Ratio			113		12.1	11.7	18.9	27.5	31.0
Net External Debt Ratio			-13.4		-5.3	1.3	11.7	20.7	21.8

COLOMBIA	1971	1972	1973	"1972"	1974	1975	1976	1977	1978
Gross Debt Service	285	315	358	319	465	471	486	484	551
Net Debt Service	276	297	334	302	400	415	421	419	428
Merchandise Exports	749	970	1262	994	1495	1717	2243	2713	3188
Gross Debt Service Ratio	38.1	32.5	28.4	32.1	31.1	27.4	21.7	17.8	17.3
Net Debt Service Ratio	36.8	30.6	26.5	30.4	26.8	24.2	18.8	15.4	13.4
Gross External Debt			2102		2370	2693	2806	3019	3361
Net Reserves			530		449	523	1161	1820	2503
Net External Debt			1572		1921	2170	1645	1199	858
Gross National Product			12078		14124	16030	17615	19685	22993
Gross External Debt Ratio			17.4		16.8	16.8	15.9	15.3	10.9
Net External Debt Ratio			13.0		13.6	13.5	9.3	6.1	3.7

IVORY COAST	1971	1972	1973	"1972"	1974	1975	1976	1977	1978
Gross Debt Service	47	61	76	61	115	132	213	286	355
Net Debt Service	39	54	68	53	99	107	203	270	331
Merchandise Exports	456	553	861	623	1214	1182	1631	2155	2323
Gross Debt Service Ratio	10.3	11.1	8.8	9.8	9.5	11.2	13.1	13.3	15.3
Net Debt Service Ratio	8.6	9.7	7.9	8.6	8.2	9.1	12.4	12.5	14.2
Gross External Debt			637		761	1016	1287	2092	3030
Net Reserves			89		66	103	77	185	448
Net External Debt			548		695	913	1210	1907	2582
Gross National Product			3655		4075	4760	5482	6305	7459
Gross External Debt Ratio			17.4		18.7	21.3	23.5	33.2	40.6
Net External Debt Ratio			15.0		17.1	19.2	22.1	30.2	34.6

MALAYSIA	1971	1972	1973	"1972"	1974	1975	1976	1977	1978
Gross Debt Service	45	61	91	66	136	138	156	249	371
Net Debt Service	-33	-13	-14	-20	-6	12	26	68	103
Merchandise Exports	1600	1680	2970	2083	4164	3771	5245	6035	7319
Gross Debt Service Ratio	2.8	3.6	3.1	3.2	3.3	3.7	3.0	4.1	5.1
Net Debt Service Ratio	-2.1	-0.7	-0.4	-1.0	-0.1	0.3	0.5	1.1	1.4
Gross External Debt			787		947	1469	1792	2223	2871
Net Reserves			1345		1618	1524	2363	2858	3329
Net External Debt			-538		-671	-75	-572	-635	-458
Gross National Product			7582		8952	10032	11692	13265	15272
Gross External Debt Ratio			10.4		10.6	14.6	15.3	16.8	18.8
Net External Debt Ratio			-7.1		-7.5	-0.7	-4.9	-4.8	-3.0

Sources : See Annex C.

Chapter IV

THE BALANCE-OF-PAYMENTS EFFECTS OF EXTERNAL SHOCKS AND OF POLICY RESPONSES IN SEVEN NON-OPEC DEVELOPING COUNTRY GROUPS

by André Barsony and Anne Richards

1. THE BALANCE-OF-PAYMENTS EFFECTS OF EXTERNAL SHOCKS

Introduction

This section contains empirical results on the balance-of-payments impact of external shocks, in the form of terms of trade effects and export volume effects, on the seven non-OPEC developing country groups, and a comparative analysis.

As noted in Chapter I, non-OPEC developing countries have been divided into seven categories depending on the level of industrialisation and the character of their principal exports (see Annex B).

Table IV-1A reports the estimated terms-of-trade and export-volume effects for each of the years 1974 to 1978 (1977 in the case of the less industrialised mineral-based countries) together with averages for the years 1974-75, 1976-77, 1974-77 and 1974-78. More detailed results are shown in Appendix Table AIV-1. In Table IV-1B, terms-of-trade effects have been related to average trade and gross national product, while export volume effects have been related to exports and to gross national product, all expressed in "1972" prices. Appendix Table AIV-2 shows the extent of export shortfalls due to the deceleration of the growth of foreign demand, and the gains (losses) resulting from increases (decreases) in export market shares for the various commodity categories. Appendix Table AIV-2 also provides information on the extent of import substitution, and on the decline of imports due to a slowdown in economic growth for each of five import categories: food, fuels, other primary products, capital goods, and other (light) manufactures.

Terms-of-Trade Effects

Group I

The newly industrialising countries (NICs) suffered substantial deterioration in their terms of trade, amounting to 41.2 per cent of the average value of their exports and imports and 5.1 per cent of GNP, on average, over the 1974-78 period. The main contributors to these terms-of-trade effects were the price increases in fuel imports and, to a lesser extent, in manufactured imports, despite important price gains in non-fuel primary exports.

As noted in Chapter II, these terms-of-trade effects can be decomposed into two parts: a pure terms-of-trade effect, calculated on the assumption of balanced trade in terms of "1972" prices; and the effects of the rise in import prices on unbalanced trade. In the 1974-78 period, on average, the pure terms-of-trade effect accounted for one-third of the total, while the effects of increased import prices on the trade deficit accounted for the remainder.

Terms-of-trade losses, which were greatest in 1975 (60 per cent of average trade and 7 per cent of GNP), declined in 1976 and 1977, largely as a result of the increased price of coffee exports as well as the decreased prices of light manufactured imports. In 1978, however, with the drop in the price of coffee, the terms-of-trade effects again worsened.

Group II

The relatively industrialised agricultural countries suffered nearly as greatly as the NICs from the effects of deteriorating terms of trade. These amounted to 33.8 per cent of average trade and 4.8 per cent of GNP, on average, in the 1974-78 period. After 1974, the pattern of terms-of-trade effects was similar to that of the NICs, with the most severe impact occurring in 1975, followed by improvements in 1976 and 1977, and a subsequent worsening in 1978. For these countries, however, the most favourable year was 1974 (rather than 1977 for the NICs) when they benefited from exceptional price increases in traditional primary exports, in particular, rice, cotton, copra and cocoanut oil.

Throughout the period, the main determinants of the terms-of-trade deterioration were the increased prices of manufactured imports and less importantly those of fuel imports instead of the reverse order experienced by the NICs. Pure terms-of-trade effects amounted to gains but only offset 4 per cent of the negative effects of the rise in import prices on the trade deficit.

Group III

The relatively industrialised mineral producing countries also suffered important terms of trade deterioration with losses representing 35.9 per cent of their average trade and 4.9 per cent of GNP, on average, in the 1974-78 period. Of these losses, around 90 per cent were due to pure terms-of-trade effects, of which the main component was the increased cost of manufactured imports, while that of fuel imports was matched by the increased earnings of non-fuel primary exports.

For these countries, the time pattern of terms of trade effects differed from that of the NICs and relatively industrialised agricultural countries. In 1974, these countries benefited from strengthened world demand for their principal exports, largely as a result of stockpiling in the developed countries. Thus, increased export prices (for copper, in particular), led to overall terms-of-trade gains in this year, amounting to 1.7 per cent of average trade and 0.2 per cent of GNP. In 1975, however, the prices of the major traditional primary exports (copper and fish meal) fell considerably, so that total terms-of-trade effects turned substantially negative, equalling 47.9 per cent of average trade and 6.7 per cent of GNP. Parallelling the price of copper, these ratios declined slightly in 1976 but rose again in 1977 and in 1978, reaching the 1975 level.

Group IV

The results for the 1974-78 period, taken as a whole, would seem to indicate that the terms-of-trade deterioration for the less industrialised agricultural countries was relatively unimportant, as it accounted for 1.5 per cent of average trade and 0.3 per cent of GNP. These results, however, mask the near equality between terms-of-trade losses in 1974, 1975 and 1978 and terms-of-trade gains in 1976 and 1977.

The largest terms-of-trade losses occurred in1975, accounting for 28.1 per cent of the average value of exports and imports and 5.3 per cent of GNP. The increased cost of manufactured imports (even greater than that of fuel imports far exceeded the improved earnings of traditional and non-traditional primary exports. In turn, 1977 was the most favourable year, with terms-of-trade gains reaching 34.5 per cent of average trade and 6.7 per cent of GNP. The quadrupling in prices of coffee and cocoa exports, which together account for one-third of total exports, essentially brought about this result. In 1978, however, the large drop in the price of coffee reversed the terms-of-trade gains. During the 1974-78 period, on average, pure terms-of-trade gains were equally matched by the negative effects of increased import prices on the trade deficit.

Group V

In comparison to the more industrialised mineral producing countries, terms-of-trade losses for these countries were less severe, although their time pattern was more irregular. In 1974, the less industrialised mineral-producing countries also benefited from increased world demand for their exports; stockpiling induced a rise in the price of copper, their principal export, which was sufficient to yield terms-of-trade gains amounting to 22.8 per cent of their average trade and 7.0 per cent of GNP. In 1975, however, these countries similarly suffered from the drop in the price of copper, which abruptly led to substantial terms-of-trade deterioration (44.7 per cent of average trade and 13.1 per cent of GNP). In the two following years, the terms-of-trade effects improved as the less industrialised countries, whose exports are concentrated on copper, coffee, and tin, benefited from the favourable price movements in these commodities; the relatively industrialised group, on the other hand, with a larger share of both manufactured exports and imports, as well as more diversified primary exports, did not experience the same improvement.

Group VI

The least developed countries suffered substantial terms-of-trade deterioration, with losses amounting to 31.3 per cent of the average value of their exports and imports and 3.8 per cent of GNP, on average, in the 1974-78 period. Since pure terms-of-trade effects represented gains, these losses were attributable to the effects of increased import prices on the trade deficit (four times larger than the gains), of which the principal component was manufactured imports.

The time pattern of terms-of-trade effects resembled that of the less industrialised agricultural countries, with large terms-of-trade gains in1977, accounting for 11.4 per cent of average trade and 1.3 per cent of GNP. The price increases in traditional primary exports (three-fourths of total exports), particularly coffee and cotton, brought about these favourable results.

Although 1975 was a comparatively bad year, as it was for the other groups, for the least developed countries, 1978 was worse, as terms-of-trade losses amounted to 60.2 per cent of average trade and 7.3 per cent of GNP. The combined effects of price increase in manufactured imports and price decreases in traditional primary exports (again coffee and cotton, in particular) were primarily responsible.

Group VII

The deterioration in the terms of trade amounted to nearly one-half the value of average trade for the group of India, Pakistan and Bangladesh in 1974-78, on average. This was the highest proportion experienced by any of the groups. As a share of GNP, however, these losses amounted to just 2 per cent – a lower proportion than for any other group (except the fourth) – reflecting the low trade share in these countries' GNP.

Like the NICS, and unlike the other groups, the main contributors to these terms-of-trade losses were the price increase in fuel imports and, to a lesser extent, that in manufactured imports.

The time pattern of terms-of-trade effects as indicated shaved peak deterioration occurring in 1975 – 68.5 per cent of average trade and 5.9 per cent of GNP – followed by improvements in 1976 and 1977 (the most favourable year) and a worsening in 1978, when the 1975 ratio was again approached. For the three South Asian countries, the 1975 and 1978 terms-of-trade losses were in large part due to the increases in the import prices of food and manufactured goods, combined with a fall in the prices of traditional primary exports, particularly cotton, vegetable oil residues and coffee. The relative improvements in 1976 and 1977, on the other hand, reflected the large increase in the price of coffee exports along with the decrease in the price of food imports.

Export Volume Effects

Group I

In 1974, the slowdown in foreign demand brought about comparatively slight shortfalls in the exports of the newly industrialising countries, amounting to 1.6 per cent of the value of exports and 0.2 per cent of GNP. In subsequent years,the shortfalls reflected the world business cycle, increasing in 1975, declining in 1976, and increasing again in 1977 and 1978, exceeding in all years the 1974 level.

For the years 1974-78, on average, export shortfalls amounted to 10.7 per cent of export value and 1.1 per cent of GNP. Manufactured goods, followed by non-traditional primary products, led the export volume losses in every year except 1974, when manufactured goods experienced volume gains.

Group II

The impact of the slowdown in foreign demand was slightly larger for the relatively industrialised agricultural countries than for the NICs, as export shortfalls amounted to 11.5 per cent of exports and 1.3 per cent of GNP, on the average, over the 1974-78 period. This result was due to the relatively greater share in their total exports of non-fuel primary products, for which the downturn in world demand was comparatively stronger than for manufactured goods.

The time pattern of these shortfalls was essentially the same as for the NICs, parallelling the world business cycle. As in the case of the NICS, manufactured exports experienced volume gains in 1974 and losses thereafter, although the largest volume losses consistently occurred in traditional primary exports, followed by non-traditional primary exports. Among traditional primary products, rice, sugar, copra, palm oil, citrus fruits and tin experienced the largest losses.

Group III

The relatively industrialised mineral-producing countries suffered comparatively small export shortfalls in 1974, as both their manufactured and traditional primary exports experienced an increase in world demand in this year. Of particular importance were the volume gains for copper due to stockpiling in developed countries.

Over the following years, the export shortfalls followed the same pattern as the world business cycle; for the years 1974-78, they averaged 10.0 per cent of exports and 1.3 per cent of GNP. Like the previous group of countries, traditional primary exports, in particular, copper, iron ore, and bauxite, experienced increasing shortfalls.

Group IV

For the less industrialised agricultural group, the slowdown in foreign demand caused export shortfalls amounting to 13.0 per cent of export value and 2.3 per cent of GNP in the 1974-78 period, on average. Traditional primary exports were responsible for three-fourths of these losses, in particular non-conifer logs, coffee, tea and bananas. In contrast, manufactured goods benefited from higher growth rates of foreing demand, with volume gains in every year between 1974 and 1977; only in 1978 did manufactured exports experience minor shortfalls. The volume gains resulted from the fact that these countries exported two-thirds of their manufactured goods to developing countries, whose demand for the manufactured exports of other developing countries accelerated.

Group V

In 1974, the mineral stockpiling policies of developed countries brought about sufficiently large export volume gains in the less-industrialised, mineral-producing countries' major export, copper, to nearly offset the shortfalls in the other exports. During the subsequent years of the period, however, export shortfalls became larger, particularly for copper and other traditional primary products, so that for the 1974-77 period, they averaged 9.8 per cent of export values and 3.2 per cent of GNP.

Unlike the relatively industrialised mineral producing countries, this group exported nearly all of their manufactured exports to developed countries, thus experiencing shortfalls in these exports throughout the period. Similar to the relatively industrialised group, however, they suffered increasing shortfalls in their traditional primary exports, most importantly, copper, iron ore and tin.

Group VI

During the years 1974-78, on average, export volume losses for the least developed countries represented 15.0 per cent of exports and 1.4 per cent of GNP. The largest part of these losses was experienced by traditional primary exports, which accounted for more than two-thirds of these countries' exports. Except for oilseed cake, sesame seeds and tobacco, the rest of the traditional primary exports suffered from the slowdown in foreign demand: cotton, bovine cattle, sheep, lambs, goats, and dried beans.

Group VII

India, Pakistan and Bangladesh experienced export shortfalls as a result of the slowdown in foreign demand, which amounted to 12.7 per cent of exports and 0.5 per cent of GNP, on average over the 1974-78 period. About three-fifths of these losses were in manufactured exports. As these countries exported a large proportion of their manufactured products to developed countries (about one-half) and to planned economies (about one-fifth), the negative effects of reduced world growth rates were more than five times greater than the positive effects of increased income elasticity of world demand for these products.

Among the other product categories, traditional primary products suffered the next largest export shortfalls, particularly jute, cotton, and iron ore.

Comparative Analysis

Apart from the less industrialised developing countries with economies based predominantly on agriculture and mineral-production, adverse terms-of-trade effects dominated adverse export volume effects in the years 1974-78, on average. This was especially true for the newly industrialising countries. During this period, the ratio of the terms-of-trade effects to the export volume effects was 4.5 for the NICs, 3.6 for the relatively industrialised agricultural group and 3.6 for the relatively industrialised mineral group. It was, respectively, 0.1, 0.9, 2.7 and 4.0 for the other four groups in numerical order, among which the countries of South Asia are the most industrialised.

The least developed countries apart, the evidence seems to indicate that, with industrialisation, developing countries become more vulnerable to terms of trade effects as their economies turn more energy-intensive and less vulnerable to export volume effects as, the proportion of manufactured exports in total exports rises. The results also show a correspondence between the level of industrialisation and the relative importance of the adverse effects of increased prices of petroleum imports as compared to manufactured imports. While the NICs and the three South Asian countries experienced relatively more unfavourable effects from the former, all other groups experienced the converse to a degree that corresponds to their level of industrialisation.

For most non-OPEC developing countries, data on manufactured exports are available in a geographical disaggregation. The data show that in the developed countries which continued to provide markets for the bulk of the developing countries' manufactured exports, an increase in the income elasticity of demand for these exports offset about one-fifth of the export shortfall due to their lower GNP growth rates. In turn, in the centrally-planned economies, a decline in the income elasticity of demand for the manufactured exports of the developing countries aggravated the adverse effects of lower GNP growth rates. Finally, in intra-LDC trade, the favourable effects of higher GNP growth rates reinforced the positive effects of increased income elasticity of demand.

Since export shortfalls are estimated as the sum of the growth and income elasticity effects, the extent of the shortfalls for each groups manufactured exports depends upon the destination of these exports. Hence, the groups which exported two-thirds or more of their manufactured exports to developed countries and essentially the remainder to developing countries (groups 1, 3, 5) obtained gains in export volumes, due to increased income elasticity, which offset about two-fifths of the volume losses, due to lower GNP growth rates. In turn, groups sending two-fifths or more of their exports to developing countries and practically the remainder to developed countries (groups 2, 4, 6) experienced gains which offset the losses by at least an half. Finally, the seventh group, which exported one fifth of their manufactured export to planned economies, minimally offset the export shortfalls.

2. THE POLICY RESPONSES AND THEIR BALANCE-OF-PAYMENTS EFFECTS

Introduction

This section presents estimates of the overall balance-of-payments effects of policy responses in the form of additional net external financing, export promotion, import substitution, and lowering the rate of economic growth as well as comparative analysis of the results.

The balance-of-payments effects of the policies applied are shown in Table IV-1A, while in Table IV-1B the results are related to the volume of exports, imports, average trade and GNP, as the case may be, all expressed in "1972" prices. More detailed estimates are provided in Appendix Tables AIV-1 and AIV-2. Table IV-2 gives a breakdown of the financing of the resource gap. Appendix Table AIV-3 provides information on the share of GDP of private and public consumption, gross domestic capital formation, increases in capital stocks and net foreign investment.

The Policies Applied

Group I

In 1974-75, on average, the balance-of-payments effects of external shocks amounted to 7.0 per cent of the NICs' GNP, in 1976-77 to 5.6 per cent, and in 1978 to 6.1 per cent. In the first two years, these countries responded to external shocks by increasing foreign borrowing to allay a deceleration in economic growth. In fact, in these years, practically the entire deterioration in the balance of payments resulting from the external shocks was financed from abroad, as savings in imports associated with slower growth and import substitution, were largely offset by decreases in export market shares.

The amounts borrowed were employed, for the most part, to finance investments in import substituting industries. After 1976, import substitution came to meet over one-half of the combined balance-of-payments effects of external shocks. Import savings due to slower growth rates were only slightly smaller, so that the NICs eliminated reliance on additional foreign borrowing. Export promotion effects remained negligible[1].

Nevertheless, borrowing in the early part of the period gave rise to an increased burden of interest payments and dividends. These outflows amounted to $5.4 billion in 1973, increased to $8.3 billion in 1974-75, to $11.0 billion in 1976-77, and to $17.3 billion in 1978. Thus, while net external financing fill from 7:1 per cent of GNP in 1974, to 0.4 per cent in 1978, the increase in combined interest payments and dividends, from 2.5 per cent to 4.8 per cent of GNP, limited the decline in total external financing from 9.7 per cent of GNP in 1974, to 5.1 per cent in 1978.

Group II

The effects of external shocks on the balance of payments of the relatively industrialised agricultural countries amounted to 6.1 per cent in 1974-78, on average. Relatively small in1974, the impact of these shocks sharply worsened in 1975, improved slightly in 1976, and deteriorated again in 1977 and in 1978, approaching the 1975 peak of 8.4 per cent of GNP.

By relying substantially on additional foreign borrowing, this group of countries was able to meet the combined adverse effects of external shocks and domestic policies as well as to sustain a higher rate of economic growth – the only group able to do so.

Although these countries increased their export market shares from 1976 to 1978, they maintained their dependence on foreign borrowing to meet the cost of increased imports associated with both their accelerated growth and increased import shares.

Interest payments and dividends rose steadily over the five-year period, from 2.1 per cent of GNP in 1974 to 3.9 per cent in 1978, raising total external financing from 4.6 per cent of GNP in 1974 to 9.0 per cent at the end of the period.

Group III

The group of relatively industrialised mineral-based countries suffered an abrupt reversal in the effects of external shocks on their balance of payments between 1974 and 1975. Shocks were favourable in 1974, due largely to increased prices of traditional primary exports. With the fall in these prices in 1975, balance-of-payments losses were substantial and remained so in the three subsequent years.

These countries, which had accumulated reserves in 1974, relied on additional net external financing to meet about three-fifths of the balance-of-payments effects of external shocks in the following years. Increases in export market shares provided the remainder as import savings due to reduced GNP growth rates were approximately offset by increased import shares.

From 1974 to 1977 interest payments and dividends rose steadily from 2.8 per cent of GNP to 4.2 per cent[2]. Total external financing, in turn, rose from 1.6 per cent of GNP in 1974 to a peak of 9.9 per cent in 1975, falling to 5.0 per cent in 1976, and increasing again to 6.8 per cent in 1977.

During the 1974-77 period, increased foreign borrowing was accompanied by a slightly higher share in GDP domestic consumption, although there were considerable year-to-year variations. A lower investment share contributed to the decline in GNP growth rates.

Group IV

In 1974-75, on average, the less industrialised agricultural countries suffered balance-of-payments losses from external shocks amounting to 5.7 per cent of GNP. To finance these losses, they relied principally on external financing and, to a much lesser extent, on import savings (from slower GNP growth rates and import substitution), which were partially offset by losses in export market shares.

1. See the discussion of this result on page 57.
2. Data for 1978 available only for Peru.

Due to substantial increases in coffee and cocoa prices, the adverse effects of external shocks declined in 1976 and gave place to gains in 1977. This improvement enabled these countries to devote their borrowed funds to increasing the share of domestic investment in GDP. The import needs of growing investment, however, led to increased import shares which were aggravated by losses in export market shares. With the effects of external shocks again negative in 1978, these countries relied on substantial additional net external financing (11.6 per cent of GNP) to meet the combined adverse effects.

Group V

Like their relatively industrialised counterpart, these mineral-based countries suffered a reversal in the balance-of-payments effects of external shocks between 1974 and 1975. In the two years following the large negative effects in 1975, however, terms of trade losses declined, mainly due to price increases in copper, the predominant export product. Nevertheless, on average, the combined effects of external shocks represented 6.1 per cent of GNP in the 1974-77 period, as compared to 5.6 per cent for the relatively industrialised group.

In addition, these countries were unable to offset the adverse balance-of-payments effects by additional foreign borrowing. As a consequence, they relied solely upon import substitution and import reductions due to greatly decreased GNP growth rates, as export market shares decreased as well. The GNP growth rate fell from 6.6 per cent during the 1963-73 period to 1.6 per cent in 1973-77, as lenders required the imposition of disinflationary measures. This was because these countries, having borrowed heavily prior to the external shocks, found themselves in 1975 with substantial interest and dividend payments, which amounted to 10.6 per cent of their GNP. With these payments gradually diminishing thereafter, total external financing, which was 18.2 per cent of GNP in 1975, declined to 9.4 per cent in 1977.

Group VI

For the least developed countries, both the pattern of external shocks and that of policy responses were similar to those for the less industrialised agricultural countries. In 1974-75, these countries experienced substantial balance-of-payments deterioration from external shocks, representing 6.4 per cent of GNP, on average. In the following two years, the impact of external shocks improved considerably, only to worsen in 1978, reaching a peak of 9.0 per cent of GNP in that year.

In response to the effects of external shocks during the first two years, the least developed countries increased their foreign borrowing as import reductions associated with import substitution and lower growth rates were more than offset by losses in export market shares. The improvements in the effects of external shocks during the next two years enabled these countries to employ their foreign resources to increase investment levels, which, in turn, led to higher import shares. With further losses in export market shares and, in particular, substantial adverse external shocks in 1978, the least developed countries substantially augmented additional net external financing, which amounted to 13.0 per cent of GNP.

Since the least developed countries received sizeable official transfers, interest payments and dividends remained around 2 per cent of GNP throughout the period, so that total external financing represented about 10 per cent of GNP in the first two years, 5 per cent in the next two, and 11 per cent in1978.

Group VII

In the South Asian countries, the balance-of-payments effects of external shocks amounted to 2.7 per cent of GNP in 1974-75, 1.8 per cent in 1976-77, and 3.0 per cent in 1978. Throughout the period, the three countries responded with increased reliance on external financing to ensure economic recovery following the 1971-72 war and the subsequent drought. In the worst years of 1975 and 1978, additional net external financing amounted to 4.8 and 5.6 per cent of GNP, respectively. This was made necessary by increases in import shares associated with the rise in investment. At the same time, the incentives for this increased investment appear to have been biased against the export sector which suffered important and successive losses in market shares. Finally, small import savings were obtained due to the fact that the growth rate in the "1972"-78 period was slightly below the 1963-73 trend rate.

Interest payments and dividends remained at around 1 per cent of GNP over the five-year period, due largely to sizeable inflows of official transfers. Correspondingly, total external financing, which amounted to 3 per cent of GNP in 1974-75, fell substantially in the following years.

Additional Net External Financing

Group I

In the 1974-78 period, on average, additional net external financing amounted to 19.9 per cent of the average value of exports and imports and 2.5 per cent of GNP in the newly industrialising countries. At the same time, the average trend value of the resource gap was 1.2 per cent of GNP, reflecting the fact that their "1972" trade deficit would have increased further if export and import trends, observed in the previous decade, had continued.

Correspondingly, the actual resource gap averaged 3.7 per cent of the NICs' GNP, expressed in terms of "1972" prices, during the 1974-78 period. Taking further account of interest payments and dividends, the ratio of total external financing to GNP was 7.0 per cent.

For the period as a whole, portfolio capital alone provided nearly three-fourths of the NICs' total external financing requirements, with foreign direct investment accounting for another one-eighth. Errors and omissions (which contain unreported capital flows) showed small outflows while there was a small accumulation of reserves.

Group II

In the relatively industrialised agricultural countries, the actual resource gap and its trend value (in surplus), respectively, averaged 3.8 per cent and 5.1 per cent of GNP in the period 1974-78, giving rise to additional net external financing of 8.9 per cent of GNP (62.4 per cent of average trade). The surplus trend value reflects the continuation of past trends in imports and exports, accompanied by large workers' remittances.

Interest and dividend charges raised total external financing to 6.9 per cent of GNP in the years 1974-78, on average. Of this amount, foreign borrowing (defined to include portfolio capital and errors and omissions) represented nearly two-thirds and foreign direct investment, about one-sixth. Except for 1975, there was a continuing accumulation of reserves.

Group III

Additional net external financing in the relatively industrialised mineral-producing countries amounted to 34.8 per cent of average trade and 4.7 per cent of GNP during the period 1974-78, on average. Net external financing averaged 1.7 per cent of GNP, while the trend resource surplus was 3.0 per cent.

Interest payments and dividends, which were almost twice as large as net external financing, brought total external financing to 7.0 per cent of GNP for the period as a whole. Most of this amount was provided by portfolio capital, while the share of direct foreign investment (about one-seventh) was offset by that of negative errors and omissions. There was little net change in reserves during the period.

Group IV

In the less industrialised agricultural countries, net external financing and its surplus trend value, respectively, averaged 3.4 per cent and 1.6 per cent of GNP, resulting in additional net external financing of 5.0 per cent (26.0 per cent of average trade) in the 1974-78 period.

As interest payments and dividends were about one-fourth larger than net external financing, total external financing amounted to 6.9 per cent of GNP during the period. Foreign direct investment met about one-seventh of total financing requirements, with portfolio capital providing the rest. Errors and omissions and reserve changes were of negligible magnitude.

Group V

In the less industrialised mineral-producing countries, the actual resource gap was less than its trend value, on average, in 1974-77, resulting in a net outflow of capital, which amounted to 0.2 per cent of GNP.

Augmented by very large interest and dividend payments, total financing requirements came to 12.5 per cent of GNP. Portfolio capital accounted for three-fourths of the total and official transfers for one-fourth. Changes in reserves were negligible but there was an outflow of other factor payments.

Group VI

For the least developed countries, additional net external financing represented 6.7 per cent of GNP and 55.2 per cent of average trade during the 1974-78 period, on average, while net external financing and its trend value, respectively, amounted to 6.6 per cent and −0.1 per cent of GNP.

The inclusion of interest and dividend payments yielded total external financing of 11.7 per cent of GNP in the same period. Portfolio capital provided about one-half and official transfers, two-fifths of the total, while small direct foreign investment inflows were offset by outflows of errors and omissions and reserve accumulation.

Group VII

Additional net external financing in India, Pakistan and Bangladesh amounted to 88.1 per cent of average trade and 3.6 per cent of GNP during the 1974-77 period, on average. The large amount of additional net external financing in 1978 (equalling 135.8 per cent of average trade and 5.6 per cent of GNP) brought the corresponding average ratios in 1974-78 to 98.7 per cent and 4.1 per cent, respectively.

For the 1974-78 period, net external financing averaged 0.6 per cent of GNP while its surplus trend value was 3.4 per cent. The surplus reflects both sizeables workers' remittances and past trends in exports and imports. At the same time, interest payments and dividends brought total external financing to 1.1 per cent of GNP. Most of this amount was provided by portfolio capital and official transfers, in nearly equal proportions.

Export Promotion

Group I

The newly industrialising countries experienced a small loss in export market shares in the 1974-78 period, on average, amounting to 0.3 per cent of their total exports, both measured in "1972" prices. For the most part, these losses occurred in traditional primary exports, as smaller losses in fuels[1] were more than offset by relatively large gains in non-traditional primary products and small gains in manufactured exports[2]. In percentage terms, actual exports fell short of hypothetical exports by 14 per cent in traditional primary exports, 19 per cent in fuels, while they exceeded hypothetical exports by 3 per cent in non-traditional primary exports, and 1 per cent in manufactured exports.

Among traditional primary exports, the greatest declines in world market shares occurred in fresh and frozen bovine meat (44 per cent), raw sugar (34 per cent), and raw cotton (31 per cent), in the period 1974-78, on average. Coffee, which accounted for one-fourth of traditional primary exports, suffered losses of 24 per cent. On the other hand, oilseed cake and iron ore experienced the greatest gains, with actual exports exceeding hypothetical exports by more than one-half.

It should be recalled that changes in export market shares are estimated as the difference between actual and hypothetical exports, both measures in "1972" prices. In the case of manufactured goods (which represent over one-half of the NIC's total exports), the hypothetical value is that which would have obtained had the NICs kept their "1972" share in all developing countries' exports of manufactured goods. As the NICs accounted for about 83 per cent of these exports in "1972", there was very little room left in subsequent years to increase their share. If, instead, the hypothetical value is computed using world manufactured exports as the norm, the result is that the NICs gained market shares for these products of 20 per cent, which would have brought total export market share gains to 8.1 per cent.

Group II

The relatively industrialised agricultural countries experienced small overall gains in export market shares, averaging 0.8 per cent of their exports in the 1974-78 period. The small gains in traditional and non-traditional primary exports and in manufactured exports (about 1 per cent each) were nearly offset by the losses in fuels (31 per cent). However, the losses in fuels were concentrated in the earlier years of the period; by 1978, actual exports had caught up with hypothetical exports, whereas in 1974 they lagged behind by 50 per cent.

1. in 1978, however, Mexico's growing oil exports provided the group with an increased share in developing countries'fuel exports.
2. While Mexico and Portugal suffered large losses in manufactured goods' market shares, the group, exclusive of these countries, experienced comparative gains in market shares in manufactured exports. Also see explanation, last paragraph of Group I.

Amounting to 0.4 per cent of total exports, on average, increases in world market shares of traditional primary products were concentrated in coffee and natural rubber. The actual exports of these two commodities exceeded their hypothetical values by 15 per cent and 4 per cent, respectively. Gains were also obtained in fresh and frozen shell fish (16 per cent), bananas (36 per cent), sugar (25 per cent), lumber (13 per cent), natural phosphates (6 per cent), palm oil (17 per cent), and coconut oil (16 per cent). In turn, losses were experienced in oranges and tangerines (17 per cent), saw and veneer logs (9 per cent), cotton (22 per cent) and tin (16 per cent), while market shares were nearly kept at their "1972" level in rice, copra and copper ores.

Group III

The relatively industrialised mineral-producing countries increased their overall market shares by 12 per cent, on average, in the 1974-78 period. Each commodity category (except fuels) experienced a gain of 13 per cent in its markets share. For fuels, however, the market share decreased by 18 per cent.

Within the traditional primary export category, copper obtained by far the largest increase in world market shares. In percentages terms, this represented a gain of 44 per cent; in value, the increase in copper's share alone raised total export earnings by 12 per cent in the years 1974-78, on average. Among the other traditional primary exports, only olive oil increased its share (7 per cent), while decreases were most important in fish meal (30 per cent) and iron ore (37 per cent). In addition, market shares declined by one-fourth in cotton, natural phosphates, bauxite, and zinc ores.

Group IV

In the less industrialised agricultural countries, the ratio of losses in export market shares to export earnings was 7 per cent in the years 1974-78, on average. The losses were divided nearly equally between non-traditional primary exports and manufactured exports, with markets shares falling 10 and 20 per cent, respectively, fuels lost 7 per cent of their "1972" share, while traditional primary exports increased their's slightly.

Largely responsible for the gains in traditional primary exports were the increases in market shares in coffee exports (27 per cent) which accounted for about one-third of the traditional primary exports of the group. Together with increases in cotton (12 per cent), these gains barely offset the declines in other traditional primary exports – fresh and frozen bovine meat (26 per cent), fresh and frozen shell fish (16 per cent), rice (14 per cent), bananas (18 per cent), cocoa beans (2 per cent), tea (6 per cent), natural rubber (6 per cent), saw and veneer logs (14 per cent), and lumber (16 per cent).

Group V

In contrast to the relatively industrialised mineral-producing countries, this less-industrialised group suffered losses in market shares, averaging 10 per cent of export value in 1974-78. Losses were experienced in every one of the export commodity categories; particularly in manufactures (about two-fifths) and in traditional primary exports (about one-third). Within the latter category, copper, this group's major export, just retained its "1972" share in world markets, while the copper exported by the relatively industrialised mineral-producing group increased its market share. At the same time, natural rubber's share declined by 19 per cent, iron ore's by 22 per cent, and that of tin by 8 per cent. Only coffee managed small gains of 9 per cent.

In 1977, overall losses in export market shares were particularly severe, amounting to 23 per cent of exports. In that year, the largest losses occurred in traditional primary products, notably, copper and iron ore.

Group VI

As a proportion of export earnings, losses in market shares were more substantial for the least developed countries than for any other group. In the years 1974-78, on average, these losses amounted to 38 per cent of exports. Moreover, similar to the other less industrialised countries, declines in total export market shares tended to worsen throughout the period. By 1978, the ratio of market share losses to exports had reached 68 per cent.

These losses in market shares were concentrated in traditional and non-traditional primary exports, while relatively small losses occurred in fuels and manufactured goods. Of the first category, only tea, groundnuts and tobacco increased their market shares, with gains representing, respectively, 23 per cent, 38 per cent, and 18 per cent. All other traditional exports lost market shares, the most important being coffee (15 per cent), cotton (25 per cent), sesame seed (15 per cent), and oilseed cake (47 per cent).

Group VII

India, Pakistan and Bangladesh also experienced substantial losses in market shares, averaging 10.3 per cent of their exports during the 1974-78 period. Substantial losses in manufactured goods (22 per cent), more than offset the gains in traditional primary exports (1 per cent) and non-traditional primary exports (11 per cent). Changes in fuels-markets were negligible.

Although the gains in non-fuel primary exports were unevenly distributed over the period, the losses in manufactured exports grew steadily over time.

Among the individual traditional primary exports, the largest gains occurred in rice (70 per cent), tea (9 per cent) and shell fish (17 per cent), and the largest losses in raw cotton (40 per cent) and iron ore (7 per cent).

Import Substitution

Group I

In the years 1974-78, on average, the newly industrialising countries experienced positive import substitution that equalled 15 per cent of their actual imports. Imports were reduced in all five categories, with actual imports falling short of hypothetical imports by one-seventh in food, fuels and other manufactures, by one-tenth in other primary products, and by a slight amount in capital goods. On the total reduction in the import bill, light manufactures accounted for one-half, food for one-sixth, and fuels, capital goods and other primary products each for about one-tenth.

Group II

In contrast to the NICs, the relatively industrialised agricultural countries experienced increased import shares, which raised their import bill by 14 per cent, on average, in the 1974-78 period. Among the individual categories, the largest increases in imports occurred in capital goods and food, providing about three-fourths and one-fourth respectively. In turn, small reductions in fuel imports were matched by increased imports of other primary products and other manufactures.

Group III

In the relatively industrialised mineral-producing group, increased import shares amounted to 6 per cent of imports in the years 1974-78, on average. Although imports of food and fuels were slightly reduced, those of other primary products, capital goods and other manufactures were substantially increased. The former represented a saving of 2 per cent on the import bill, while the latter increased it by 8 per cent, of which other primary products and capital goods contributed one-half each.

Group IV

The less industrialised agricultural countries also experienced increased import-shares, which raised their import bill by 8 per cent, on average, in 1974-78. Among individual commodity categories, increased income elasticities of import demand led to an excess of actual over hypothetical imports by 28 per cent in other primary products, 16 per cent in capital goods, 7 per cent in fuels, and 2 per cent in other manufactures. In turn, the fall in the income elasticity of demand for food imports brought about a 15 per cent decline in actual food imports as compared to hypothetical imports.

Group V

Import substitution reduced imports by one-fifth in the less industrialised mineral-producing countries in 1974-77, on average – the largest reduction experienced by any of the groups. Of this total, the largest components were capital goods (43 per cent), food (27 per cent) and other manufactures (19 per cent), with the remainder in fuels (9 per cent) and other primary products (2 per cent).

Group VI

In the years 1974-78, on average, import substitution amounted to 10 per cent of actual imports in the least-developed countries. Decreased income elasticities of import demand brought actual imports below hypothetical imports by 40 per cent in fuels, about 15 per cent in other primary products and other manufactures, and 10 per cent in food. The opposite occurred for capital goods, where actual imports surpassed hypothetical imports by 3 per cent.

Group VII

India, Pakistan and Bangladesh experienced larger increased import shares than any of the other groups, averaging 30 per cent of imports in the 1974-78 period. In the aftermath of the 1971-72 war and the subsequent drought, India and Pakistan increased their import demand, in particular, for capital goods and other manufactures. Actual imports of these commodities were almost twice and three times larger than they would have been in the event of unchanged income elasticities of import demand. There was also an increased share of food imports alongside a decreased share of fuels and other primary products.

Lowering Economic Growth Rates

Group I

Another form of policy response to adverse external shocks is temporarily to lower the rate of economic growth by the use of deflationary monetary and/or fiscal policies. This was the case in the newly industrialising countries as their average GNP growth rates from "1972" to 1978 were lower than in the 1963-73 period.

Lower GNP growth rates, in turn, reduced imports. Estimated as the positive difference between trend and hypothetical imports, the effects of slower growth calculated for each of the five import categories by relating income elasticities of import demand, estimated for the 1963-73 period, to GNP growth rates in that period and in the period under study, respectively. In the years 1974-78, on average, the overall excess of trend over hypothetical imports represented 12 per cent of actual imports. Among the individual categories, reductions in the imports of capital goods and other manufactured goods, respectively, contributed nearly one-third and over two-fifths to the overall import reduction, with food, fuels and other primary products each accounting for about one-tenth.

Group II

The relatively industrialised agricultural countries were the only group to increase their economic growth rates, thereby increasing their imports by 3 per cent in the years 1974-78, on average. Capital goods and light manufactures, in particular, represented the bulk of the increase.

Group III

The relatively industrialised mineral-producing countries experienced reductions in imports from slower GNP growth rates amounting to 6 per cent of imports in 1974-78, on average. The largest reductions occurred in light manufactures and food, with fuels, capital goods, and other primary products accounting for the remainder.

Group IV

The less industrialised agricultural countries experienced comparatively small import reductions due to lower GNP growth rates, amounting to 2 per cent of imports in the 1974-78 period, on average. Capital goods provided almost three-fifths and other manufactured goods, the remainder of the import savings.

Group V

In the years 1974-77, on average, the less industrialised mineral-producing countries reduced their imports 17 per cent by slowing their economic growth. Capital goods and other manufactures shared the largest reductions, accounting for nearly one-half and one-third of overall import savings, respectively.

Group VI

Lower growth rates in the least developed countries induced import savings equal to 4 per cent of imports in 1974-78, on average. Among individual categories, other manufactures provided one-third of overall savings, capital goods and fuels each about one-fourth, food nearly one-fifth, and other primary products only a small fraction.

Group VII

In the three South Asian countries "1972"-78 GNP growth rates were only slightly below the average rate for the 1963-73 period. Thus, import savings represented only 1.5 per cent of imports in 1974-78, on average, with capital goods and other manufactures accounting for most of the total.

Comparative Analysis

Comparison of the balance-of-payments effects of additional net external financing with those of the internal policy measures of export promotion, import substitution, and the deceleration of economic growth reveals considerable differences among the seven groups of countries. At one extreme, additional net external financing was approximately one-and-a-half to two times as large as the adverse effects of external shocks in all the predominantly agricultural groups, including the least developed countries and the countries of South Asia. At the other extreme, a net outflow of capital, resulting from constrained financial market accessibility, imposed wholly internal adjustment in the less industrialised mineral-producing countries. In between these extremes, a combination of foreign borrowing and internal adjustment was used in the relatively industrialised mineral-producing countries and the NICs, with additional net external financing meeting three-fourths of the adverse effects of external shocks in the case of the former group but only two-fifths in the case of the latter.

Considerable differences were also shown in the use of the various internal policy measures in response to balance-of-payments deterioration from external shocks. With respect to export promotion, only the relatively industrialised mineral-producing countries increased their export market shares: the NICs and the relatively industrialised agricultural producers experienced little change, and the less industrialised groups incurred substantial losses.

Import substitution had positive effects in the NICs, the less industrialised mineral-producing countries, and the least developed countries. Among the other groups, in contrast, increased import shares were largest in the agricultural countries and the countries of South Asia, whereas they were comparatively unimportant in the relatively industrialised mineral-producing countries.

The policy of reducing imports by deflationary policies was used, in particular, by the less-industrialised mineral-producing countries, whose only alternative was import substitution. For the other groups of countries, however, the effects of macroeconomic policies were relatively weak.

The impact of the two import-reducing policies was greatest, for every group of countries, on manufactured imports. While reductions were largest in light manufactures by the NICs, the least developed and South Asian countries, capital goods imports were curtailed most substantially by every other country group.

Comparing the five-year pattern of policy responses to external shocks across the seven groups reveals important differences between the newly industrialising countries and the rest. While the former were increasingly able to supplant additional net external financing with the effects of internal adjustment policies (in particular, export promotion and import substitution), the latter remained dependent upon additional net external financing to meet the combined adverse balance-of-payments effects of external shocks, export market share losses and increased import shares. Only in the case of the fifth group, which was unable to increase their foreign borrowing sufficiently, were substantial import substitution and deflationary measures taken.

A further difference exists between the more industrialised and the less industrialised groups, apart from the fifth, in which the balance-of-payments effects of internal policies, albeit-negative, declined over time in the more industrialised groups while they increased in the less industrialised groups.

Tabl[e]

BALANCE OF PAYMENTS EFFECTS OF EXTERNAL SHOCKS AND OF POLICY RESPO[NSES]

Balance of Payments Effects	Explanations	1974	1975	1976	1977	1978	1974-75 Average	1976-77 Average	1974-77 Average	1974-78 Average	1974	1975
		NEWLY INDUSTRIALISING COUNTRIES									RELATI[VE]	
I. External Shocks												
(1) Terms-of-trade Effects	See text	16872	22532	17874	12322	15107	19702	15098	17400	16941	1128	5250
(2) Export Volume Effects of Changes in Foreign Demand	in "1972" prices	467	3775	2302	5443	6942	2121	3873	2997	3786	450	1123
(3) Together		17339	26307	20176	17764	22048	21823	18971	20397	20727	1578	6373
II. Policy Responses												
(4) Additional Net External Financing	See text	19651	18123	8721	-1747	- 3935	1887	3487	11187	8163	3839	8210
(5) Increase in Export Market Share	in "1972" prices	-1471	-520	-965	179	2200	-996	-393	-694	-116	-421	-149
(6) Import Substitution	idem	-571	5889	8028	10297	12252	2659	9163	5911	7179	-1668	-1484
(7) Import Effects of Lower GNP Growth Rates	idem	-270	2815	4392	9036	11530	1273	6714	3993	5501	-171	-204
(8) Together		17339	26307	20176	17764	22048	21823	18971	20397	20727	1578	6373
III. Aggregate Values												
(9) Exports	in "1972" prices	29737	30644	35378	37597	42920	30191	36488	33339	35255	8508	8674
(10) Imports	idem	48816	44667	46256	45971	48924	46742	46114	46428	46927	12481	12823
(11) Average Trade	(9) + (10) :2	39277	37656	40817	41784	45922	38467	41301	39884	41091	10495	10749
(12) Gross National Product	in "1972" prices	308703	316692	330404	344635	360799	312698	337520	325109	332247	71297	76131
		LESS INDUSTRIALISED COUNTRIES WITH ECONOMIES BASED PREDOMINANTLY ON MINERAL PRODUCTION										
I. External Shocks												
(1) Terms-of-Trade Effects	See text	-571	1064	300	143	..	246	222	234	..	365	744
(2) Export Volume Effects of Changes in Foreign Demand	in "1972" prices	16	318	290	412	..	167	351	259	..	101	116
(3) Together		-556	1382	590	555		413	573	493		466	861
II. Policy Responses												
(4) Additional Net External Financing	See text	-811	940	-146	-37		65	-92	-13		604	1014
(5) Increase in Export Market Share	in "1972" prices	-106	-135	-298	-543		-121	-421	-271		-350	-289
(6) Import Substitution	idem	267	300	618	573		283	596	439		229	109
(7) Import Effects of Lower GNP Growth Rates	idem	95	277	416	562		186	489	338		-17	27
(8) Together		-556	1382	590	555		413	573	493		466	861
III. Aggregate Values												
(9) Exports	in "1972" prices	2825	2638	2655	2409		2732	2532	2632		994	1074
(10) Imports	idem	2182	2118	1821	1891		2150	1856	2003		1449	1599
(11) Average Trade	(9) + (10) :2	2504	2378	2238	2150		2441	2194	2318		1222	1337
(12) Gross National Product	in "1972" prices	8149	8120	8179	8096		8135	8138	8136		10286	10384

Source : See Annex C.

- 1B

EXTERNAL SHOCKS AND OF POLICY

: RATIOS (in per cent)

1974	1975	1976	1977	1978	1974-1975	1976-1977	1974-1977	1974-1978	1974	1975	1976	1977	1978	1974-1975	1976-1977	1974-1977	1974-1978
Relatively Industrialised Countries with economies based predominantly on mineral production									Less Industrialised Countries with economies based predominantly on agriculture								
-1.7	47.9	41.7	41.9	47.4	23.5	41.8	32.8	35.9	14.5	28.1	-3.6	-34.5	6.4	21.4	-19.7	0.1	1.5
-0.2	6.7	5.5	5.8	6.6	3.2	5.6	4.4	4.9	2.8	5.3	-0.7	-6.7	1.2	4.1	-3.8	0.02	0.3
0.9	11.3	9.1	12.9	15.2	6.0	11.1	8.6	10.0	6.2	11.2	8.4	19.8	20.3	8.7	13.8	11.3	13.0
0.1	1.5	1.2	1.8	2.1	0.8	1.5	1.1	1.3	1.2	2.1	1.5	3.2	3.1	1.6	2.4	2.0	2.3
-0.1	8.2	6.7	7.5	8.7	4.0	7.1	5.6	6.2	4.0	7.5	0.9	-3.5	4.3	5.7	-1.4	2.0	2.5
10.4	54.1	41.2	39.9	46.5	22.4	40.5	31.6	34.8	20.8	31.5	5.7	8.8	60.0	26.2	7.3	16.4	26.0
-1.4	7.6	5.4	5.5	6.5	3.0	5.5	4.3	4.7	4.0	6.0	1.1	1.7	11.6	5.0	1.4	3.1	5.0
10.2	12.3	5.4	12.2	14.6	11.3	9.0	10.1	11.1	-2.3	1.5	-5.5	-11.5	-17.5	-0.4	-8.3	-4.3	-6.9
-0.8	-10.8	-2.4	-5.4	-9.0	-6.1	-4.0	-5.0	-5.8	0.8	3.7	0.9	-17.7	-21.9	2.3	-9.4	-4.0	-8.4
0.2	3.9	6.5	8.1	10.4	2.1	7.3	4.7	5.9	1.2	2.6	3.2	2.8	2.2	1.9	3.0	2.5	2.4
South Asian Countries																	
47.0	68.5	35.6	29.5	52.4	58.4	32.5	44.8	46.5									
1.9	2.9	1.5	1.2	2.2	2.4	1.3	1.9	1.9									
2.1	13.2	8.5	16.1	22.3	7.9	12.2	10.2	12.7									
0.1	0.5	0.4	0.6	0.8	0.3	0.5	0.4	0.5									
2.0	3.4	1.8	1.8	3.0	2.7	1.8	2.2	2.4									
75.7	114.2	69.2	92.0	135.8	96.0	80.8	88.1	98.7									
3.1	4.8	2.9	3.8	5.6	4.0	3.3	3.6	4.1									
-11.7	-2.7	-2.6	-13.7	-20.5	-7.1	-8.0	-7.6	-10.3									
-14.5	-30.1	-23.8	-34.6	-43.0	-22.9	-29.5	-26.3	-30.1									
-0.2	1.9	1.4	2.1	2.1	0.9	1.7	1.3	1.5									

TABLE [cut off]

FINANCING THE EXTERNAL RESOURCE G[cut off]

	1971	1972	1973	"1972"	1974	1975	1976	1977	1978
	Newly Industrialising Countries								
Interest Receipts	1123	1371	2106	1533	3414	2591	2322	2793	6057 a/
Interest Payments	-3099	-3701	-5320	-4040	-7633	-8638	-9675	-11526	-17104 a/
Dividends	-9	-5	-43	-19	-202	-189	-468	-263	-162
Other Factor Payments	-522	1167	1962	869	2675	3220	1729	1488	2509
Official Transfers	115	139	876	377	773	692	1287	988	1204
Direct Investment	1398	1629	2951	1993	3230	2955	2902	3142	4114
Portfolio Capital	4582	6196	7316	6031	16001	17855	20295	16088	15904
Errors and Ommissions	623	1395	115	711	-18	-1292	-2007	-1648	1323
Changes in Reserves	-2509	-7090	-6129	-5243	3722	3376	-4524	-5548	-12584
Net External Financing	1702	1101	3834	2212	21962	20570	11861	5514	1261
Total External Financing b/	4810	4807	9197	6271	29797	29397	22004	17303	18527 a/
	Less Industrialised Countries with economies based predominantly on mineral production								
Interest Receipts	68	55	68	64	111	82	152	110	
Interest Payments	-319	-448	-557	-442	-677	-701	-564	-532	
Dividends	-64	-95	-97	-86	-148	-159	-69	-66	
Other Factor Payments	-128	-142	-167	-146	-235	-261	-254	-267	
Official Transfers	267	453	352	357	452	475	502	628	
Direct Investment	135	225	261	207	299	74	93	79	
Portfolio Capital	210	508	137	285	545	869	930	539	
Errors and Ommissions	-213	-212	-281	-235	-406	-103	-137	-114	
Changes in Reserves	300	129	-157	91	-217	342	13	-219	
Net External Financing	255	473	-442	95	-277	619	666	159	
Total External Financing b/	639	1016	213	622	548	1478	1299	757	

	1971	1972	1973	"1972"	1974	1975	1976	1977	1978
	Relatively Industrialised Countries with economies based predominantly on agriculture								
Interest Receipts	108	101	173	127	422	547	448	511	696
Interest Payments	-633	-693	-1007	-357	-1363	-1405	-1746	-2022	-2490
Dividends	-76	-102	-51	-76	-101	-340	-964	-1190	-1189
Other Factor Payments	118	229	349	232	721	431	1137	350	1729
Official Transfers	529	186	230	315	237	215	142	141	209
Direct Investment	264	261	441	322	913	798	707	1233	1370
Portfolio Capital	1234	1706	307	1082	1874	1900	3976	5057	5987
Errors and Ommissions	-21	-133	102	-17	-37	-342	-277	1433	-891
Changes in Reserves	-494	-1447	-1848	-1263	-835	930	-1296	-425	-1499
Net External Financing	1029	108	-1304	-56	1831	2734	2127	5088	3922
Total External Financing b/	1738	903	-246	798	3295	4479	4837	8300	7601
	Least Developed Countries								
Interest Receipts	26	26	47	33	58	53	61	46	74 a/
Interest Payments	-77	-88	-100	-88	-118	-135	-137	-110	-98 a/
Dividends	-33	-38	-48	-40	-52	-53	-49	-63	-44
Other Factor Payments	10	33	14	19	9	16	-18	23	7
Official Transfers	54	91	136	94	282	399	214	342	311
Direct Investment	14	-17	45	14	60	43	16	12	24
Portfolio Capital	228	218	235	227	554	507	273	355	453
Errors and Ommissions	-14	-42	-41	-32	-41	-31	-90	-9	212
Changes in Reserves	39	-112	-160	-78	44	124	-7	-198	181
Net External Financing	247	71	128	149	796	976	263	398	1120
Total External Financing b/	357	197	276	277	966	1164	449	571	1262 a/

Sources: See Annex C

Notes:
a/ Includes earnings (payments) on other goods, services and income.
b/ Net external financing plus interest payments and dividends.
c/ Available only for Peru.

- 2

($ million in current prices)

1971	1972	1973	"1972"	1974	1975	1976	1977	1978
Relatively Industrialised Countries with economies based predominantly on mineral production								
62	49	78	63	138	113	77	69	34 c/
-297	-310	-393	-333	-609	-721	-868	-1008	-2951 a/
-144	-182	-156	-161	-87	-97	-110	-100	-18 c/
-47	-18	-96	-53	-154	-88	-42	-84	1587 a/
55	54	79	63	46	89	124	123	104
75	152	198	142	-426	422	294	133	265
147	172	602	307	1476	1310	966	1688	1360
-77	-90	-116	-94	-218	-283	-367	-93	233
45	32	-199	-41	-470	813	187	-122	-576
-181	-141	-2	-108	-305	1559	261	605	38
260	351	546	386	391	2376	1239	1714	-
South Asian Countries								
61	53	78	64	130	166	227	308	355
-423	-425	-476	-441	-392	-517	-493	-603	-648
-49	-15	-16	-27	16	-24	1	-6	16
-52	-61	-25	-46	-45	0	13	38	151
259	207	403	290	2400	709	688	700	890
0	21	-17	1	-2	15	0	15	36
1187	465	841	831	-112	2056	1730	1295	1263
-123	-231	-56	-137	-288	-474	-305	-317	-2
-89	33	184	42	311	-75	-2265	-1540	-1935
771	47	916	578	2018	1856	-404	-110	126
1243	487	1408	1046	2394	2397	88	499	758

1971	1972	1973	"1972"	1974	1975	1976	1977	1978
Less Industrialised Countries with economies based predominantly on agriculture								
40	60	60	53	88	108	83	100	83 a/
-103	-155	-232	-163	-278	-268	-300	-452	-353 a/
-152	-105	-160	-139	-116	-257	-293	-357	-385
-39	-69	-130	-79	-134	-239	-289	-356	-429
215	282	201	233	245	323	257	328	284
73	55	89	72	107	220	122	113	178
300	90	529	306	764	820	762	1475	1937
-7	-12	0	-6	-66	40	-6	-2	-167
91	-64	-148	-40	88	244	-203	-842	-131
418	82	209	236	698	991	133	7	1017
673	342	601	539	1092	1516	726	816	1755 a/

Annex A

ESTIMATING CHANGES IN THE BALANCE OF PAYMENTS

THE ANALYTICAL FRAMEWORK

by Bela Balassa

In developing the analytical framework designed to examine the balance-of-payments effects of external shocks and of policy responses to these shocks, the point of departure is the balance-of-payments identity. This is defined in terms of the resource gap that equals the deficit in merchandise trade and in non-factor service items combined, with further adjustment made for private transfers; the resource gap is financed by the net flow of external financing.

The resource gap is shown in equations 1) and 2) for years 0 and 1, respectively. In the equations, M and X denote merchandise imports and exports, valued in base year (0) prices; $P_{01}{}^{m}$ and $P_{01}{}^{x}$ represent percentage changes in import and export prices between years 0 and 1; and S and R refer to the balance of non-factor services and private transfers and to the resource gap, respectively, valued in terms of current prices.

1) $$R_0 = M_0 - X_0 - S_0$$

2) $$R_1 = M_1\,(1+P_{01}{}^{m}) - X_1\,(1+P_{01}{}^{x}) - S_1$$

Taking the difference between equations 2) and 1) and rearranging terms, we express changes in the resource gap between years 0 and 1 in equation 3) in terms of changes in import and export prices for the volume of imports and exports in period 1$(P_{01}{}^{m}M_1 - P_{01}{}^{x}X_1)$; changes in the volume of imports $(M_1 - M_0)$; changes in the volume of exports $(X_1 - X_0)$; and changes in the balances of non-factor services and private transfers $(S_1 - S_0)$.

3) $$R_1 - R_0 = (P_{01}{}^{m}\,M_1 - P_{01}{}^{x}\,X_1) + (M_1 - M_0) - (X_1 - X_0) - (S_1 - S_0)$$

Equation 3) is modified if we examine the effects of policy equations taken at home and abroad. As a first step, we introduce hypothetical exports $(X_1{}^{h})$ that would be reached if the country in question maintained its base-year share in world markets. Now, differences between actual and hypothetical exports $(X_1 - X_1{}^{h})$, shown on the left-hand side of equation 4), are taken to have resulted from domestic policy actions as regards exports.

4) $$(R_1 - R_0) + (X_1 - X_1{}^{h}) = (P_{01}{}^{m}M_1 - P_{01}{}^{x}X_1) + (M_1 - M_0) - (X_1{}^{h} - X_0) - (S_1 - S_0)$$

Next, we introduce the effects of changes in foreign demand. For this purpose, we calculate the trend value of exports $(X_1{}^{t})$ on the assumption that the trend of foreign export demand remained the same as in the base period and the country under consideration maintained its export share unchanged. The difference between trend and hypothetical values $(X_1{}^{t} - X_1{}^{h})$, shown on the right-hand side of equation 4), thus represents the effects of the external shock due to changes in foreign demand on the country's exports. (Since this export shortfall adds to the deficit, it is shown with a positiv sign.)

5) $$(R_1 - R_0) + (X_1 - X_1{}^{h}) = (P_{01}{}^{m}M_1 - P_{01}{}^{x}X_1) + (X_1{}^{t} - X_1{}^{h}) + (M_1 - M_0) - (X_1{}^{t} - X_0) - (S_1 - S_0)$$

In turn, hypothetical imports $(M_1{}^{h})$ are calculated for the actual growth rate of GNP in the country concerned on the assumption that the income elasticity of import demand remained the same as in the base period. Differences between hypothetical imports $(M_1{}^{h})$ and actual imports (M_1), shown in equation 6), are taken to reflect the effects of import-substituting policies.

6) $$(R_1 - R_0) + (X_1 - X_1{}^{h}) + (M_1{}^{h} - M_1) = (P_{01}{}^{m}M_1 - P_{01}{}^{x}X_1) + (X_1{}^{t} - X_1{}^{h}) + (M_1{}^{h} - M_0) - (X_1{}^{t} - X_0) - S_1 - S_0)$$

Furthermore, we calculate the trend value of imports on the assumptions that the income elasticity of import demand and the rate of growth of GNP remained the same as in the base period (i.e. no change in the rate of growth of imports). Differences between the trend value of imports and hypothetical imports $(M_1^t - M_1^h)$, shown on the left-hand side of the equation 7), are assumed to reflect the effects of changes in the rate of growth of GNP on imports.

7) $$(R_1 - R_0) + (X_1 X_1^h) + (M_1^h - M_1) + (M_1^t - M_1^h) = (P_{01}^m M_1 - P_{01}^x X_1) + (X_1^t - X_1^h) + (M_1^t - M_0) - (X_1^t - X_0) - (S_1 - S_0)$$

The difference between the trend values for imports and exports adjusted for the actual balance of non-factor services and private transfers equals the amount of net external financing that would have been necessary in the absence of external shocks and policy responses to these shocks (the trend value of the resource gap, R_1^t). In turn, the sum of differences between trend values and actual values of imports and exports equals the difference between the trend value of the resource gap and its actual value in the base year.

Introducing the trend value of the resource gap and rearranging terms, we show the excess of the actual resource gap over its trend value on the left-hand side of equation 8). This is taken to represent the additional inflow of external funds associated with the balance-of-payments effects of external shocks (additional net external financing).

8) $$(R_1 - R_1^t) + (X_1 - X_1^h) + (M_1^h - M_1) + (M_1^t - M_1^h) = (P_{01}^m M_1 - P_{01}^x X_1) + (X_1^t - X_1^h) + (M_1^t - M_0) - (X_1^t - X_0) - (S_1 - S_0) - (R_1^t - R_0)$$

The last term on the right-hand side of equation 9) equals the sum of the previous three terms and indicates the amount of additional external financing that would have been necessary in the absence of external shocks if exports and imports assumed their trend values and non-factor services and private transfers their actual values, over and above the inflow of external funds in the base year. The term is shown with a negative sign, so that the last four terms add up to zero and can be omitted.

Under the assumption that the country in question is a price-taker in world markets, the right-hand side of equation 8) is taken to indicate the effects of external shocks on the balance of payments. This is decomposed into effects on the terms of trade $(P_{01}^m M_1 - P_{01}^x X_1)$ and on export volume $(X_1^t - X_1^h)$. The former is further decomposed into a pure terms of trade effect, calculated on the assumption of balanced trade in base year prices $(P_{01}^m - P_{01}^x) X_1$, and the effects of increased import prices on unbalanced trade, $(M_1 - X_1) P_{01}^m$.

In turn, the left-hand side of equation 8) consists of terms representing policy reactions to external shocks, including additional net external financing $(R_1 - R_1^t)$, increases in the country's export share in world markets $(X_1 - X_1^h)$, import substitution $(M_1^h - M_1)$, and the effects of lower GNP growth rates on the country's imports $(M_1^t - M_1^h)$.

In the case of manufactured exports, the effects of lower growth rates of GNP abroad and the effects of changes in the foreign income elasticity of demand for these exports have further been distinguished. This has involved calculating the constant-price-value of the exports of manufactured goods by developing countries to developed countries, developing countries, and centrally planned economies that would have been obtained if the income elasticity of import demand in these areas remained the same as in the base period (X_{m1}^{c}).

Assuming further that the country in question maintained its share in the manufactured exports of the developing countries unchanged, the difference between the trend value of manufactured exports and the constant-income-elasticity value of the exports of manufactured goods $(X_{m1}^{t} - X_{m1}^{c})$ is taken to reflect the effects of changes in GNP growth rates abroad. In turn, the difference between constant-income-elasticity exports and hypothetical exports $(X_{m1}^{c} - W_{m1}^{h})$ represents the effects of changes in foreign income elasticities of demand for the manufactured exports of the developing countries. Again, a positive sign denotes an export shortfall.

Annex B

A TYPOLOGY OF NON-OPEC DEVELOPING COUNTRIES

by André Barsony
with the assistance of Anne Richards

This typology is an attempt to group non-OPEC developing countries (with populations **larger than one million**) according to similar structural characteristics (industrialisation level and nature of principal exports in 1973). Data difficulties were encountered at two levels requiring the exclusion of several countries first from the typology and second from the analysis. In the following tables, countries which are underlined are those included in the external shocks methodology while countries with an asterisk are those included in the analysis of the debt situation.

The non-OPEC developing countries were grouped as follows: First, the Newly Industrialising Countries (see Table B1) were distinguished by their high share of manufacturing in both GDP and total exports. Second, the Least Developed Countries (see Table B6) were identified as those countries belonging to the internationally-recognised list. Finally, the ramaining countries were classified first by the predominance of agricultural or mineral production (and their related manufactures) in both GDP and total exports. These two groups were then sub-divided into countries which were relatively more or less industrialised, using a benchmark of 15 per cent of manufacturing in GDP (see Tables B2 through B5).

In addition to these categories, a seventh category has been established, combining India, Pakistan and Bangladesh to form a seventh group. Due to the large size of these countries within their respective groups, to their 1971-72 war and subsequent drought, as well as to the inseparability of the data for Bangladesh and Pakistan prior to 1972, it was felt that these countries possessed greater similarities with respect to each other than within their respective groups where their presence would have biased the results for the group as a whole.

In several cases, countries did not fit neatly in any category as defined by the criteria and some judgment was relied upon for their classification. These cases are indicated at the bottom of the Tables under "Exceptions".

TABLE B1

NEWLY INDUSTRIALISING COUNTRIES

	% GDP in 1973			% Total exports in 1973			Industrial origin of manufactured exports in 1973									GNP/c in 1973	Population in 1973	"1972" Share in group's total exports	"1972" Share in group's total imports
	Man.	Ag.	M & Q	Man.	Ag.	M & Q	Food, bev., tob.	Tex-tiles	Wood & prod.	Paper & prod.	Chem. ind.	Non-metal min.	Basic metal	Metal manuf.	Other man. ind.		(000s)	%	%
*Argentina	29	14	1	66	34	.2	40	8	0	1	4	.3	4	9	.2	1640	24,282	9	5
*Brazil	24	9	.5	54	38	8	29	8	3	1	3	.4	2	6	2	760	101,051	17	13
*Greece	18	18	1	71	24	5	15	17	.6	.4	20	1	13	4	.7	1870	8,930	4	7
Hong Kong	28	2	.1	99	.9	.6	1	52	.4	1	5	.3	.5	23	16	1430	4,160	--	--
Israel	20[c]	5	c	47	12	41	7	10	.7	1	9	.2	2	10	7	3010	3,210	5	8
*Korea	26	25	1	93	6	1	4	43	10	2	5	1	6	17	5	400	32,905	8	8
Mexico	23	11	3	64	32	5	10	8	.7	1	8	2	11	20	2	890	56,047	7	8
Portugal	31	15	.4	89	4	7	16	30	8	5	8	3	1	17	1	1410	8,994	5	6
*Singapore	24	2	.2	76	23	.7	6	8	6	1	25	.4	1	26	3	1830	2,185	10	10
*Spain	26	11	1	85	14	.9	16	13	1	3	12	2	7	28	2	1710	34,740	15	18
*Taiwan	40	13	.9													660	15,424	12	7
*Uruguay	20	17	.4	80[b]	19[b]	.5[b]	68[b]	12[b]	--	--	.2[b]	.5[b]	--	--	--	950	2,995	1	1
*Yugoslavia	39[d]	19	d	91	7	2	11	15	7	2	8	1	16	31	1	1010	20,956	9	9

Criteria: 1. Share of manufacturing in GDP ⩾ 25 per cent in 1973.
2. Share of manufacturing in total exports ⩾ 50 per cent in 1973.

Exceptions: Greece, Israel, Uruguay. Although these countries do not meet the first criterion, nor Israel the second, the predominance of manufacturing in exports, together with their high GNP per capita place them in this category.
(a) 1974 (b) 1972 (c) manufacturing + mining and quarrying (d) manufacturing + mining and quarrying + electricity, gas and water (e) 1971 (f) 1975 (g) manufacturing + electricity, gas and water (h) 1969 (i) 1970 (j) 1976.

Sources: UN, Monthly Bulletin of Statistics, various issues; UN, Yearbook of International Trade Statistics, 1978; World Bank Tables, 1973.

TABLE B2

RELATIVELY INDUSTRIALISED DEVELOPING COUNTRIES WITH ECONOMIES BASED PREDOMINANTLY ON AGRICULTURE (AND RELATED MANUFACTURES)

	% GDP in 1973			% Total exports in 1973			Industrial origin of manufactured exports in 1973									GNP/c in 1973	Population in 1973	"1972" Share in group's total exports	"1972" Share in group's total imports
	Man.	Ag.	M & Q	Man.	Ag.	M & Q	Food, bev., tob.	Tex-tiles	Wood & prod.	Paper & prod.	Chem. ind.	Non-metal min.	Basic metal	Metal manuf.	Other man. ind.		(000s)	%	%
*Columbia	18	32	1	31	60	9	7	9	1	.9	7	1	1	3	.3	440	22,500	11	12
*Costa Rica	19	19	.2	43	57	0	19	4	.7	1	9	.1	2	5	3	710	1,872	3	5
*Philippines	25	29	2	49	33	18	28	2	8	.7	2	1	2	.7	5	280	40,219	16	19
*Egypt	16	29	.9	38	54	9	10	20	0	.4	4	1	1	2	.1	250	35,619	11	11
El Salvador	18	28	.2	42	57	.3	10	14	0	3	7	.2	2	5	.7	350	3,771	--	--
Guatemala	15[f]	28[f]	0[f]	45	55	.2	17	9	1	2	9	2	1	3	.4	500	5,175	--	--
*Malaysia	15	33	5	45	52	3	10	2	12	.2	4	.2	13	4	.7	570	11,302	25	23
Morocco	15	27	9[f]	38	35	27	20	8	.6	1	4	.3	.2	2	.3	320	15,903	8	11
Nicaragua	21	25	.5	50	48	2	29	5	3	.4	8	1	.6	2	.1	540	1,973	--	--
Paraguay	16	38	.2	72	28	0	52	2	9	0	8	.1	--	0	0	410	2,416	--	--
*Thailand	16	34	1	48	48	4	21	9	3	.2	2	1	7	.9	5	270	39,400	14	20
*Turkey	19	25	1	34	63	3	12	12	.4	.1	5	2	2	1	.2	600	37,930	11	20

Criteria:
1. Share of manufacturing in GDP 15 ≤ 24 per cent in 1973.
2. Share of agriculture in GDP ≥ 25 per cent in 1973.
3. Share of agriculture and related manufactures in total exports ≥ 50 per cent in 1973.

Exceptions: Costa Rica, Philippines. While the Philippines exceed the first criterion, their predominant share of agriculture in GDP, together with their low GNP/c, place them in this category. Costa Rica does not meet the second criterion but because of it's predominant share of agriculture (not including related manufactures) in total exports, it is placed in this category.

(a), (b) ... (i) see Table B1

TABLE B3

RELATIVELY INDUSTRIALISED DEVELOPING COUNTRIES WITH ECONOMIES BASED PREDOMINANTLY ON MINERAL PRODUCTION (anD RELATED MANUFACTURES)

	% GDP in 1973			% Total exports in 1973			Industrial origin of manufactured exports in 1973									GNP/c in 1973	Population in 1973	"1972" Share in group's total exports	"1972" Share in group's total imports
	Man.	Ag.	M & Q	Man.	Ag.	M & Q	Food bev. tob.	Tex-tiles	Wood & prod.	Paper & prod.	Chem. ind.	Non-metal min.	Basic metal	Metal manuf.	Other man. ind.		(000s)	%	%
*Chile	32	7	11	86	2	12	2	0	1	3	2	0	77	.7	0	720	10,230	38	34
*Jamaica	16	7	9	68	8	23	16	2	0	.4	47	.5	.4	2	.3	990	1,967	14	21
*Peru	23[b]	16[b]	7[b]	65	15	20	24	2	.2	.2	5	.2	33	.5	.2	620	14,531	36	29
*Tunisia	11	19	8	51	9	40	25	4	.5	2	12	.7	6	1	.2	460	5,459	12	17

Criteria: 1. Share of manufacturing in GDP ⩾ 15 per cent in 1973.
2. Share of mining and quarrying in GDP 5 ⩽ 15 per cent in 1973.
3. Share of mining and quarrying and related manufactures in total exports ⩾ 50 per cent in 1973.

Exceptions: **Tunisia.** **Tunisia does not meet the first criterion, however, its relatively diversified manufacturing sector and high GNP/c place it in this group.**

Note: **South Africa would have been placed in this group but the fact that its substantial gold exports are not recorded in trade data necessitated South Africa's exclusion.**

a) b) ...i) see Table B1.

TABLE B4

LESS INDUSTRIALISED DEVELOPING COUNTRIES WITH ECONOMIES BASED PREDOMINANTLY ON AGRICULTURE (AND RELATED MANUFACTURES)

	% GDP in 1973			% Total exports in 1973			Industrial origin of manufactured exports in 1973									GNP/c in 1973	Population in 1973	"1972" Share in group's total exports	"1972" Share in group's total imports
	Man.	Ag.	M & Q	Man.	Ag.	M & Q	Food, bev., tob.	Tex-tiles	Wood & prod.	Paper & prod.	Chem. ind.	Non-metal min.	Basic metal	Metal manuf.	Other man. ind.		(000s)	%	%
*Burma	9	39	2	38	51	11	22	0	9	0	3	--	4	0	.1	80	29,509	5	6
*Cameroon	13	32	.2	27	73	0	9	2	4	.1	1	.2	7	3	0	250	6,206	10	11
*Ghana	12	49	2[b]	26	70	4	9	.1	9	0	.8	0	7	.2	.1	300	9,313	18	14
*Honduras	14	31	2	34	57	9	11	2	16	.4	3	.7	.3	.7	0	320	2,781	9	8
*India	13	45	.8	62	27	11	12	36	.1	.3	3	.6	3	6	2	120	581,911	--	--
*Ivory Coast	14	28	.3	26	74	.3	10	2	5	.3	4	.2	.5	3	.7	380	5,887	24	19
*Kenya	11	29	.4	38	61	.4	14	2	.9	1	16	3	.1	2	.2	170	12,480	15	21
*Madagascar	13	32	2[e]	32	64	4	18	3	.1	.1	9	.2	.3	2	.1	--	8,301	7	8
*Pakistan	14	33	.7	86	14	.7	21	57	0	.1	1	1	.1	3	2	120	66,230	--	--
*Sri Lanka	10	33	1	13[b]	86[b]	1[b]	7[b]	.7[b]	.1[b]	0[b]	1[b]	0[b]	0[b]	0[b]	4[b]	120	13,180	14	14

Criteria:
1. Share of manufacturing in GDP 10 < 15 per cent in 1973.
2. Share of agriculture in GDP ⩾ 25 per cent in 1973.
3. Share of agriculture and related manufactures in total exports ⩾ 50 per cent in 1973.

Exceptions: India, Pakistan. These countries do not meet the third criterion. However, their predominant share of agriculture in GDP and their low levels of manufacturing in GDP and GNP/c place them in this category.

a) b)....i) see Table B1

TABLE B5

LESS INDUSTRIALISED DEVELOPING COUNTRIES WITH ECONOMIES BASED PREDOMINANTLY ON MINERAL PRODUCTION (AND RELATED MANUFACTURES)

	% GDP in 1973			% Total exports in 1973			Industrial origin of manufactured exports in 1973									GNP/c in 1973	Population in 1973	"1972" Share in group's total exports	"1972" Share in group's total imports
	Man.	Ag.	M & Q	Man.	Ag.	M & Q	Food, bev., tob.	Tex-tiles	Wood & prod.	Paper & prod.	Chem. ind.	Non-metal min.	Basic metal	Metal manuf.	Other man. ind.		(000s)	%	%
*Bolivia	12	15	17	51	5	44	3	.1	.8	0	2	.6	44	.4	0	230	5,331	8	9
*Liberia	4	25	28	3	21	76	.8	.3	0	0	.5	0	0	.8	.5	310	1,452	10	8
*Mauritania	5	22	33	8[b]	10[b]	81[b]	3[b]	.1[b]	0[b]	0[b]	0[b]	0[b]	0[b]	5[b]	0[b]	200	1,257	4	4
*Papua New Guinea	6	26	26	8	29	63	4	0	3	0	.4	0	0	.2	.2	410	2,596	11	15
*Sierra Leone	8	28	17	3	21	76	2	0	0	--	1	--	--	.2	.1	160	2,787	4	6
*Zaire	8	17	22	79	12	10	6	0	.7	0	.3	.1	70	.5	.5	140	23,438	30	29
*Zambia	12	11	33	99	1	.2	.1	0	0	0	0	0	98	.4	.1	430	4,646	32	29

Criteria:
1. Share of manufacturing in GDP ≤ 15 per cent in 1973.
2. Share of mining and quarrying in GDP > 15 per cent in 1973.
3. Share of mining and quarrying and related manufactures in total exports > 50 per cent in 1973.

a) b) ...i) see Table B1.

TABLE B6

LEAST DEVELOPED COUNTRIES

	% GDP in 1973			% Total exports in 1973			Industrial origin of manufactured exports in 1973									GNP/c in 1973	Population in 1973	"1972" Share in group's total exports	"1972" Share in group's total imports
	Man.	Ag.	M & Q	Man.	Ag.	M & Q	Food, bev., tob.	Tex-tiles	Wood & prod.	Paper & prod.	Chem. ind.	Non-metal min.	Basic metal	Metal manuf.	Other man. ind.		(000s)	%	%
Afghanistan	19^{fd}	56^{fd}	^{fd}	18	71	12	5	11	--	--	0	0	--	--	2	90	16,634	--	--
Bangladesh	7^{c}	60	^{c}	69^{f}	32^{f}	0^{f}	$.3^{f}$	65^{f}	0^{f}	1^{f}	$.7^{f}$	0^{f}	--	$.7^{f}$	$.5^{f}$	80	74,000	--	--
*Benin	9^{d}	32	^{d}	29	71	.1	16	5	.1	.2	.5	.3	.2	5	1	110	2,947	--	--
*Central Afr. Repu.	9^{g}	32^{e}	6^{e}	18	51	31	2	2	13	--	.8	0	0	.4	0	160	1,710	3	3
*Chad	11^{f}	41^{f}	$.8^{f}$	28	72	.5	12	2	0	0	11	.1	0	1	.5	80	3,873	--	--
*Ethiopia	9	47	.2	27	72	.3	23	1	.2	.2	1	.6	--	.5	.6	90	26,550	13	13
*Haiti	11^{f}	45^{f}	1^{f}	42	46	13	11	11	2	0	8	--	--	2	8	130	4,454	--	--
*Malawi	9	49	.1	15	85	0	12	1	.5	.1	.4	0	0	.7	.5	110	4,833	6	8
*Mali	--	--	--	20^{b}	80^{b}	$.7^{b}$	7^{b}	10^{b}	$.2^{b}$	0^{b}	$.4^{b}$	$.2^{b}$	0^{b}	1^{b}	1^{b}	70	5,370	3	5
*Niger	6^{h}	51^{h}	$.1^{h}$	28	33	39	20	4	0	0	.1	--	0	3	1	100	4,357	--	--
*Rwanda	4	61	1	6	73	21	3	--	--	--	--	--	--	2	.5	70	3,980	--	--
*Somalia	--	--	--	17	84	0	14	.1	0	0	.1	0	0	1	.8	80	3,042	3	5
*Sudan	9	41	.3	16	85	.1	14	.6	--	0	1	0	--	.2	0	130	17,051	28	25
*Tanzania	10	35	1	16	77	8	6	3	.6	0	5	.1	.1	.2	.1	130	13,974	24	28
*Uganda	8^{a}	62^{a}	$.7^{a}$	10	90	.2	4	.5	.1	0	0	.2	5	0	0	150	10,829	21	13
*Upper Volta	10^{a}	41^{a}	$.1^{a}$	16	84	0	9	4	0	0	.8	.1	.2	2	.5	70	5,714	--	--
Yemen A.R.	2	61	.7	22	78	.1	19	1	--	--	.1	--	--	.5	1	100	6,217	--	--

Criteria: Although these countries belong to the internationally recognised list of Least Developed Countries (those for whom data is available for classification and with populations greater than 1 million) following the above criteria they may be placed in the fourth group. (Only Bangladesh does not meet the third criterion yet may nonetheless be placed in this group due to its predominant share of agriculture in GDP and low GNP/c). What distinguishes these countries from the others in the fourth group is their low GNP/c.

a) b) ...i) see Table B1.

TABLE B7

SOUTH ASIAN COUNTRIES

	% GDP in 1973			% Total Exports in 1973			Industrial origin of manufactured exports in 1973									
	Man.	Ag.	M & Q	Man.	Ag.	M & Q	Food bev, tob	Tex-tiles	Wood & prod.	Paper & prod.	Chem. ind.	Non-metal min.	Basic metal	Metal manuf.	Other man. ind.
India	13	45	.8	62	27	11	12	36	.1	.3	3	.6	3	6	2
Pakistan	14	33	.7	86	14	.7	21	57	0	.1	1	1	.1	3	2
Bangladesh	7[c]	60	[c]	69[f]	32[f]	0[f]	.3	65[f]	0[f]	1[f]	.7[f]	0[f]	..	.7[f]	.5[f]

	GNP/c in 1973	Population in 1973	"1972" Share in group's total exports	"1972" Share in group's total imports
			%	%
		(000s)	(Share in group excluding India and Pakistan)	
India	120	581,911	73	68
Pakistan	120	66,230	21	20
Bangladesh	80	74,000	6	12

Note: While India and Pakistan have been categorised in the fourth group and Bangladesh, in the sixth, these countries have been analysed as a separate group due to their large size within their respective groups, to their 1971-72 war and subsequent drought, as well as to the inseparability of the data for Bangladesh and Pakistan prior to 1972.

Annex C

APPENDIX TABLES TO CHAPTERS III AND IV

List of Sources

Balance of Payments Effects of External Shocks and

($ mi

	1974	1975	1976	1977	1974–75	1976–77	1974–77	1974
	B R A Z I L							
I. EXTERNAL SHOCKS								
Effects of Increased Import Prices	6222	6453	7143	7170	6338	7157	6748	3136
of which, Fuels	2611	2743	3400	3588	2677	3494	3086	778
Non-fuels	3611	3710	3743	3582	3661	3663	3662	2358
Effects of Increased Export Prices	3094	3161	4479	6344	3128	5412	4270	1498
of which, Traditional Primary	1666	1582	2519	3361	1624	2940	2282	52
Fuels	86	155	197	173	121	185	153	79
Other Non-traditional Primary	724	722	934	1494	723	1214	969	164
Manufactured	618	702	829	1316	660	1073	866	1203
Services								0
Private Transfers								
Difference (Terms of Trade Effects)	3128	3292	2664	826	3210	1745	2478	1638
of which, Price Terms of Trade Effect	709	1818	1654	460	1264	1057	1161	1002
Unbalanced Trade Effect	2419	1474	1010	366	1945	688	1317	636
Trend Value of Exports, in "1972" prices	4932	5260	5619	6020	5096	5820	5458	2585
Hypothetical Exports, idem	4753	4730	5305	5250	4742	5278	5010	2477
Difference (Export Volume, Effects)	179	530	314	770	355	542	449	108
of which, Traditional Primary	137	323	232	487	230	360	295	39
Fuels	2	14	12	17	8	15	11	1
Other Non-traditional Primary	60	92	66	116	76	91	84	11
Manufactured	-20	101	4	150	41	77	59	57
of which, Growth Effects	57	192	214	285	125	249	187	182
Income Elasticity Effects	-77	-91	-210	-135	-84	-173	-129	-125
Services								0
Private Transfers								
II. POLICY RESPONSES								
Actual Resource Gap in General Prices	6277	4913	3818	1649	5595	2734	4164	2053
Trend Value of Resource Gap in "1972" Prices	1708	2162	2996	3973	1935	3485	2709	1363
Difference (Additional Net External Financing)	4569	2751	822	-2324	3660	-751	1455	690
Actual Exports in "1972" Prices	4857	5509	5649	5776	5183	5714	5449	2963
Hypothetical Exports, idem	4753	4730	5305	5250	4742	5278	5010	2477
Difference (Increase in Export Market Share)	104	779	344	526	442	435	439	486
of which, Traditional Primary	-253	94	-79	-132	-80	-106	-93	24
Fuels	-30	-2	0	-11	-16	-6	-11	4
Other Non-traditional Primary	163	313	314	398	238	356	297	46
Manufactured	224	374	109	271	299	190	245	414
Services								-2
Private Transfers								
Hypothetical Imports in "1972" Prices	7204	7872	9021	9695	7538	9358	8448	4597
Actual Imports, Idem	7946	7139	6583	6087	7543	6335	6939	3716
Difference (Import Substitution)	-742	733	2438	3608	-5	3023	1509	881
of which, Fuels	205	229	224	310	217	267	242	81
Non-Fuels	-947	504	2214	3298	-222	2756	1267	800
Trend Value of Imports, in "1972" Prices	6580	7431	8395	9481	7006	8938	7972	4286
Hypothetical Imports, idem	7204	7872	9020	9695	7538	9357	8448	4597
Difference (Import Effects of Lower GNP Growth Rate)	-624	-441	-625	-214	-532	-419	-476	-311
of which, Fuels	-71	-52	-73	-32	-61	-52	-57	-27
Non-Fuels	-553	-389	-552	-182	-471	-367	-419	-284

Source : National and International Trade Statistics.

TABLE A III-Ia

of Policy Responses to These Shocks : Related Data

lion)

1975	1976	1977	1974-75	1976-77	1974-77	1974	1975	1976	1977	1974-75	1976-77	1974-77
K O R E A						T U N I S I A						
3442	4057	5124	3290	4591	3940	498	706	699	845	602	772	687
1043	1341	1714	911	1528	1219	98	103	128	150	101	139	120
2399	2716	3410	2379	3063	2721	400	603	577	695	501	633	567
1678	2938	4882	1589	3910	2749	638	657	550	686	647	618	632
108	99	350	80	224	152	189	156	79	50	172	64	118
79	111	95	79	103	91	234	251	239	282	242	261	251
182	174	389	173	282	227	19	32	27	36	26	32	29
1306	2434	3675	1255	3055	2155	131	105	86	143	118	114	116
3	120	373	2	246	124	51	87	90	132	69	111	90
						14	26	29	43	20	36	28
1764	1119	242	1701	681	1191	-140	49	149	159	-45	154	55
1389	1382	365	1196	874	1035	-168	-12	36	-40	-90	-2	-46
375	-263	-123	505	-193	156	28	61	113	199	45	156	101
2962	3399	3905	2774	3652	3213	616	677	740	808	646	775	709
2465	3187	3243	2471	3215	2843	573	583	634	645	578	640	608
497	212	662	303	437	370	43	94	106	163	68	135	101
57	55	61	48	58	53	19	59	57	67	39	62	51
6	5	8	3	6	5	3	4	0	5	3	2	3
23	17	27	17	22	20	3	25	22	31	14	27	20
413	138	569	235	354	294	-4	9	4	15	3	10	6
548	606	786	365	696	530	5	13	20	28	9	24	16
-135	-468	-217	-130	-342	-236	-9	-4	-16	-13	-6	-14	-10
-2	-3	-3	-1	-3	-2	23	-1	15	36	11	26	18
						-1	-2	8	9	-2	8	3
1954	611	55	2004	333	1168	-43	161	361	482	59	422	240
1886	2417	3175	1625	2796	2210	-33	-82	-91	-121	-58	-106	-82
68	-1806	-3120	379	-2463	-1042	-10	243	453	603	117	528	322
3414	5023	5823	3189	5423	4306	592	650	694	746	621	720	670
2465	3187	3243	2471	3215	2843	573	583	634	645	578	640	608
949	1836	2580	718	2208	1463	19	67	60	101	43	80	62
117	46	165	71	106	88	12	-12	-8	-16	0	-12	-6
4	10	2	4	6	5	4	8	3	10	6	7	7
151	51	188	98	119	109	-5	34	-5	6	14	0	7
674	1610	1947	544	1778	1161	2	-13	23	71	-6	47	21
3	119	278	1	199	100	-11	30	34	17	10	25	17
						17	20	13	13	19	13	16
5445	7154	8796	5021	7975	6498	546	596	640	665	571	652	612
3832	4717	5687	3774	5202	4488	627	712	827	976	670	901	786
1613	2437	3019	1247	2773	2010	-81	-116	-187	-311	-99	-249	-174
76	140	202	79	171	125	2	4	5	7	3	6	4
1537	2297	2907	1169	2602	1885	-83	-120	-192	-318	-102	-255	-178
5076	6018	7131	4681	6575	5628	571	545	569	595	533	582	558
5445	7154	8796	5021	7975	6498	546	596	640	665	571	652	612
-369	-1136	-1665	-340	-1401	-870	-25	-51	-71	-70	-38	-70	-54
-34	-93	-136	-31	-115	-73	-6	-10	-15	-21	-8	-18	-13
-335	-1043	-1529	-310	-1286	-798	-19	-41	-56	-49	-30	-52	-41

Appendix Tabl

Balance of Payments Effects of External Shocks and of Polic

	1974	1975	1976	1977	1974-75	1976-77	1974-77	197
	M	E	X	I	C O			
I - External Shocks								
Effects of Increased Import Prices	1706	2245	2160	2378	1976	2268	2122	81
of which, Fuels	300	234	239	106	267	173	220	16
Non-Fuels	1406	2011	1921	2272	1709	2097	1902	64
Effects of Increased Export Prices	1334	1664	1962	2451	1500	2206	1853	51
of which, Traditional Primary	288	230	572	631	279	601	440	43
Fuels	86	314	427	803	215	615	415	2
Other Nontraditional Primary	276	217	207	353	247	280	263	2
Manufactured	325	341	442	702	333	572	453	3
Services	125	166	130	76	146	103	124	
Private Transfers	234	326	184	-114	280	35	158	
Difference (Terms of Trade Effects)	372	581	198	-73	476	62	269	29
of which, Pure Terms of Trade Effect	-473	-762	136	1295	-618	715	49	-29
Unbalanced Trade Effect	845	1343	-62	-1368	1094	-653	220	59
Trend Value of Exports in "1972" Prices	4277	4655	5075	5540	4466	5308	4887	102
Hypothetical Exports, idem	4379	4151	4706	4769	4265	4738	4501	128
Difference (Export Volume Effects)	-102	504	369	771	201	570	386	-26
of which, Traditional Primary	83	95	92	120	89	106	98	-26
Fuels	1	7	6	9	4	8	6	
Other Nontraditonal Primary	30	36	28	48	33	38	35	
Manufactured	-17	109	52	164	46	108	77	
of which, Growth Effects	45	169	177	223	107	200	154	
Income Elasticity Effects	-62	-60	-125	-59	-61	-92	-47	-
Services	5	2	-24	52	3	14	9	
Private Transfers	-206	255	215	378	25	297	161	
II - Policy Responses								
Actual Resource Gap In Current Prices	1633	2451	1473	-84	2042	695	1368	61
Trend Value of Resource Gap in "1972" Prices	399	290	292	1010	320	651	485	-9
Difference (Additional Net External Financing)	2032	2741	1765	926	2362	1246	1853	70
Actual Exports, in "1972" Prices	3744	3450	3830	4328	3598	4079	3838	99
Hypothetical Exports, idem	4379	4151	4706	4769	4265	4738	4501	128
Difference (Increase in Export Market Shares)	-635	-701	-876	-441	-667	-659	-664	-29
of which, Traditional Primary	-110	-168	-179	-204	-139	-192	-165	-30
Fuels	8	90	101	197	49	149	99	-
Other Nontraditional Primary	15	-29	-122	-90	-7	-106	-57	-
Manufactured	63	-128	-322	-223	-35	-272	-153	2
Services	-22	-205	-234	-149	-113	-192	-153	
Private Transfers	-589	-261	-120	28	-425	-46	-235	
Hypothetical Imports, in "1972" Prices	3215	3303	3337	3433	3259	3385	3322	115
Actual Imports, idem	4351	4335	3870	3512	4343	3691	4017	148
Difference (Import Substitution)	-1136	-1032	-533	-79	-1084	-306	-695	-32
of which, Fuels	82	117	124	168	100	146	123	
Non-Fuels	-1218	-1149	-657	-247	-1184	-452	-818	-33
Trend Value of Imports, in "1972" Prices	3222	3380	3548	3725	3301	3637	3469	110
Hypothetical Imports, idem	3215	3303	3337	3433	3259	3385	3322	115
Difference (Import Effects of Lower GNP Growth Rate)	7	77	211	292	42	252	147	-5
of which, Fuels	1	10	27	38	5	33	19	1
Non-Fuels	6	67	184	254	37	219	128	-6

A III - Ib

Responses to These Shocks. Related Data ($ million)

1975	1976	1977	1974-75	1976-77	1974-77	1974	1975	1976	1977	1974-75	1976-77	1974-77
	P E R U					P O R T U G A L						
1339	1271	1335	1075	1303	1189	1779	1714	1794	2142	1747	1968	1857
228	261	272	198	267	232	371	432	496	528	402	513	457
1111	1010	1063	877	1037	957	1408	1282	1298	1614	1345	1455	1400
384	396	530	448	463	455	1371	1204	998	1257	1288	1128	1207
314	303	385	374	344	359	201	146	133	137	174	134	154
33	41	41	27	41	34	38	25	24	21	31	23	27
19	23	43	20	33	27	67	39	-9	0	53	-4	24
18	28	62	27	45	36	507	435	323	455	471	389	430
						177	141	133	169	159	151	155
						381	418	394	475	400	435	417
955	875	805	627	840	734	408	510	796	885	459	840	650
-152	464	705	-225	584	180	314	579	540	512	446	526	486
1107	411	100	852	256	554	94	-69	256	373	13	314	164
1048	1078	1114	1035	1096	1065	3161	3436	3743	3348	2979	3331	3155
723	663	836	1003	750	876	3062	2896	3315	4093	3299	3918	3608
325	415	278	32	346	189	99	540	428	745	320	587	453
312	411	261	25	336	180	6	42	20	40	24	30	27
2	2	3	1	2	2	1	6	5	8	4	6	5
4	0	5	3	3	3	9	13	1	17	11	10	11
6	2	9	3	5	4	5	184	39	257	95	148	121
9	10	14	6	12	9	88	280	310	406	184	358	271
-3	-8	-5	-3	-7	-5	-83	-96	-271	-149	-89	-210	-150
						77	100	108	124	88	116	102
						1	195	255	299	98	277	187
330	880	552	972	716	844	754	558	1161	893	656	1027	842
-153	-173	-198	-124	-186	-155	-207	-244	-319	-772	-225	-546	-385
483	1053	750	1096	902	999	961	802	1480	1665	881	1573	1227
907	964	1196	950	1081	1015	2536	2153	2117	2311	2345	2213	2279
723	663	836	1003	750	876	3062	2896	3315	3348	2979	3331	3155
184	301	360	-53	331	139	-526	-743	-1198	-1037	-634	-1118	-876
206	315	345	-48	330	141	-51	-82	-53	-44	-66	-48	-57
2	3	1	-1	2	0	3	-8	-11	-13	-3	-12	-7
-5	-4	0	-5	-2	-3	-27	10	10	16	-8	13	2
-19	-13	14	1	1	1	-201	-378	-767	-749	-290	-758	-524
						-62	-187	-236	-213	-124	-225	-175
						-188	-98	-141	-34	-143	-88	-115
195	1213	1202	1175	1207	1191	2607	2429	2667	2892	2518	2779	2649
529	1249	1262	1505	1255	1380	2678	2070	2467	2797	2374	2632	2503
-334	-36	-60	-330	-48	-189	-71	359	200	95	144	147	146
-15	-12	-34	-5	-23	-14	-19	-13	-13	2	-16	-6	-11
-319	-24	-26	-325	-25	-175	-52	372	213	93	160	153	157
142	1185	1234	1122	1210	1167	2750	3061	3409	3799	2906	3604	3255
195	1213	1202	1175	1208	1191	2607	2429	2667	2892	2518	2779	2649
-53	-28	32	-53	2	-26	143	632	742	907	388	825	606
29	48	74	22	61	41	2	24	24	27	13	26	19
-82	-76	-42	-75	-59	-67	141	608	717	880	375	799	587

APPENDIX TABLE

BALANCE OF PAYMENTS EFFECTS OF EXTERNAL SHOCKS AND OF POLICY

	1974	1975	1976	1977	1974-75	1976-77	1974-77
	COLOMBIA						
I - External Shocks							
Effects of Increased Import Prices	468	534	663	853	501	758	630
of which Fuels	3	11	33	107	7	70	39
Non-Fuels	465	522	630	746	494	688	591
Effects of Increased Export Prices	421	375	802	1563	398	1183	790
of which Traditional Primary	179	178	571	1225	179	898	539
Fuels	87	79	54	75	83	65	79
Other Non traditional Primary	30	20	35	61	25	48	37
Manufactured	125	97	141	202	111	157	134
Services							
Private Transfers							
Difference (Terms of Trade Effects)	47	159	-139	-710	103	-425	-161
of which Pure Terms of Trade Effect	- 8	230	-205	-924	111	-565	-227
Unbalanced Trade Effect	55	-71	65	217	- 8	140	66
Trend Value of Exports, in "1972" prices	1018	1081	1151	1228	1050	1190	1120
Hypothetical Exports, idem	960	992	1071	1008	976	1040	1008
Difference (Export Volume Effects)	59	89	80	221	74	151	112
of which Traditional Primary	69	60	63	174	65	119	92
Fuels	2	18	16	23	10	20	15
Other Non traditional Primary	3	3	3	5	3	4	4
Manufactured	-15	9	- 2	20	- 3	9	3
of which Growth Effects	8	38	40	52	23	46	35
Income Elasticity Effects	-24	-30	- 42	- 32	-27	- 37	- 32
Services							
Private Transfers							
II - Policy Responses							
Actual Resource Gap in Current Prices	168	-183	-543	-723	- 8	-633	-321
Trend Value of Resource Gap, in "1972" Prices	-45	-291	-636	-496	-168	-566	-367
Difference (Additional Net External Financing)	213	108	93	-227	161	- 67	47
Actual Exports in "1972" Prices	996	1090	943	880	1043	912	978
Hypothetical Exports, idem	960	992	1071	1008	976	1040	1008
Difference (Increase in Export Market Shares)	36	98	-128	-127	67	-128	- 30
of which Traditional Primary	63	206	7	0	135	4	35
Fuels	-44	- 39	- 57	- 53	- 42	- 55	- 49
Other Non traditional Primary	9	0	9	27	5	18	12
Manufactured	8	- 69	- 87	-101	- 31	- 94	- 63
Services							
Private Transfers							
Hypothetical Imports in "1972" Prices	996	1007	1023	1042	1002	1033	1017
Actual Imports, idem	1129	961	1047	1175	1045	1111	1078
Difference (Import Substitution)	-133	46	- 23	-134	- 44	- 78	- 61
of which Fuels	4	1	- 6	- 27	3	- 16	- 7
Non fuels	-137	45	- 18	-107	- 46	- 62	- 54
Trend Value of Imports, in "1972" Prices	986	1003	1022	1041	995	1032	1013
Hypothetical imports, idem	996	1007	1023	1042	1002	1033	1017
Difference (Import Effects of Lower GNP Growth Rate)	- 10	- 4	- 1	- 1	- 7	- 1	- 4
of which Fuels	1	1	0	0	1	0	1
Non fuels	- 11	- 5	- 2	1	- 8	- 1	- 5

A III - Ic

RESPONSES TO THESE SHOCKS. RELATED DATA ($ million)

974	1975	1976	1977	1974-75	1976-77	1974-77	1974	1975	1976	1977	1974-75	1976-77	1974-77
I V O R Y C O A S T							M A L A Y S I A						
290	427	555	862	359	709	534	1501	1421	1582	1932	1461	1757	1609
100	117	126	156	109	141	125	272	301	382	436	287	409	348
190	310	429	706	250	568	400	1229	1120	1200	1496	1174	1348	1261
415	427	768	1420	421	1094	758	1844	1407	2396	3202	1626	2800	2213
329	299	653	1208	374	931	623	1274	744	1349	1878	1009	1614	1312
22	40	36	54	31	45	38	262	313	587	664	288	625	456
40	48	51	112	44	81	63	126	131	172	265	129	219	174
24	40	28	46	32	37	35	184	219	288	395	200	342	271
125	0	-213	-558	-62	-385	-224	-343	14	-814	-1270	-165	-1043	-604
11	55	- 22	-538	22	-315	-147	-470	241	-342	-1068	-115	- 706	-411
114	-55	-121	- 20	-85	- 70	- 77	127	227	-472	- 202	- 50	- 337	-193
726	769	815	866	748	841	796	2343	2488	2647	2821	2416	2734	2575
664	642	710	667	653	689	671	2255	2146	2404	2386	2201	2395	2298
62	127	105	199	95	152	124	88	342	243	435	215	339	277
57	111	99	180	84	140	112	78	267	219	336	173	278	225
1	3	3	4	2	3	3	5	40	37	51	22	44	33
6	9	3	8	8	6	7	18	24	0	31	21	15	18
2	4	0	7	1	3	2	-13	11	-13	17	-1	2	1
2	7	8	12	4	10	7	11	40	45	61	26	53	40
4	- 3	- 8	- 5	- 3	- 7	-5	-24	-29	-58	-44	-27	-51	-39
60	150	- 46	-222	45	-134	-44	3	185	-1120	-1201	94	-1160	-533
221	167	264	281	194	273	234	-251	80	- 124	- 213	-85	- 168	-127
281	-17	-310	-503	-149	-407	-278	254	105	- 996	- 988	179	- 992	-408
838	812	967	992	825	980	903	2390	2440	2899	2876	2415	2887	2651
664	642	710	667	653	689	671	2255	2146	2404	2386	2201	2395	2298
174	170	257	325	172	291	232	135	294	495	490	214	492	353
117	84	155	94	100	125	113	44	125	243	235	84	239	161
11	15	15	16	13	15	14	- 70	-40	14	25	-55	19	- 18
40	43	76	190	42	133	87	83	66	97	105	74	101	88
7	28	10	25	17	18	18	78	143	141	125	111	133	122
607	629	711	760	618	736	677	2496	2485	2717	2970	2491	2843	2667
604	718	794	970	661	832	772	2610	2104	2232	2604	2357	2418	2388
3	-89	-83	-210	- 43	-146	-95	-114	381	485	366	134	425	279
- 9	-10	- 6	- 8	- 10	- 7	- 9	21	43	35	27	32	31	32
12	-79	-77	-202	- 33	-139	86	-135	338	450	339	102	394	247
648	692	739	789	670	764	717	1966	2061	2162	2267	2014	2214	2114
607	629	711	760	618	736	677	2496	2485	2717	2970	2491	2483	2667
41	63	28	29	52	28	40	- 50	-424	-555	-703	-477	-629	-553
2	3	1	2	3	1	2	- 6	- 5	- 5	- 5	- 6	- 5	- 5
39	60	27	27	49	27	38	-524	-419	550	-698	-471	-624	-548

Appendix - Table A III-2

Trade Effects of External Shocks and of Policy Responses to These Shocks: Merchandise Trade
(1974-77 Average)

EXPORTS	Brazil	Korea	Tunisia	Mexico	Peru	Portugal	Colombia	Ivory Coast	Malaysia
Traditional Primary Products									
Hypothetical / Trend	90.8	68.6	69.0	87.2	81.1	92.4	86.7	81.6	87.7
Actual / Hypothetical	96.7	176.2	94.5	77.0	117.8	82.6	111.6	123.0	110.3
Fuels									
Hypothetical / Trend	83.0	83.0	82.8	83.2	83.1	83.2	83.1	81.5	83.4
Actual / Hypothetical	80.3	120.9	107.6	439.6	106.9	58.2	32.8	221.7	88.8
Non-traditional Primary Products other than fuels									
Hypothetical / Trend	90.9	90.7	92.7	91.2	92.1	91.7	91.3	94.1	92.7
Actual / Hypothetical	134.9	158.3	117.8	84.8	91.3	93.5	131.6	183.3	137.8
Manufacturing Goods									
Hypothetical / Trend	96.0	89.5	93.1	92.6	93.4	92.5	99.1	97.4	99.8
Actual / Hypothetical	120.2	146.2	124.2	83.0	104.2	65.0	79.7	124.8	136.2
Total									
Hypothetical / Trend	91.8	88.4	80.6	90.5	82.6	92.3	90.0	84.4	89.2
Actual / Hypothetical	108.8	148.0	108.5	86.6	121.6	70.1	97.0	134.6	115.4
IMPORTS									
Fuels									
Hypothetical/ Trend	105.7	117.2	134.3	90.1	64.7	90.6	91.8	94.1	103.3
Actual / Hypothetical	78.0	74.9	92.0	30.1	118.1	105.8	255.6	126.1	81.2
Non-fuels									
Hypothetical / Trend	106.3	115.4	107.5	96.1	106.4	80.8	100.5	94.3	128.0
Actual / Hypothetical	85.2	68.6	132.3	126.0	115.7	93.6	105.3	112.7	90.4
Total									
Hypothetical / Trend	106.0	115.5	109.7	95.8	102.1	81.4	100.4	94.4	126.2
Actual / Hypothetical	82.1	69.1	128.4	120.9	115.9	94.5	106.0	114.0	89.5

Source: National and International Trade Statistics.

Appendix Table IV-1

Balance-of-Payments Effects of External Shocks and of Policy Responses to these Shocks: Related Data

	1974	1975	1976	1977	1978	1974-75	1976-77	1974-77	1974-78
	Newly Industrialising Countries								
I. External Shocks									
Effects of Increased Import Prices	35223.7	40486.4	43350.4	48589.7	61916.0	37855.1	45970.1	41912.6	45913.2
of which: Food	4721.5	5228.4	4115.2	4430.2	5503.3	4975.0	4272.7	4623.8	4799.7
Fuels	11162.5	12100.9	14970.3	16062.5	17887.5	11631.7	15516.4	13574.1	14436.7
Other Primary Products	4310.9	3198.5	3864.4	5044.2	6002.9	3754.7	4454.3	4104.5	4484.2
Capital Goods	4603.3	8477.4	9721.9	11234.3	17043.0	6540.4	10478.1	8509.2	10216.0
Other Manufactures	10425.5	11481.2	10678.6	11818.5	15479.3	10953.4	11248.6	11101.0	11976.6
Effects of Increased Export Prices	18351.8	17954.5	25476.6	36268.1	46809.4	18153.2	30872.4	24512.8	28972.1
of which: Traditional Primary Products	2679.3	2190.5	3469.4	4149.8	3204.9	2434.9	3809.6	3122.3	3138.8
Non-traditional Primary Products	5474.5	4870.6	6472.2	9913.6	11365.5	5172.6	8192.9	6682.7	7619.3
Fuels	2213.8	2433.9	2756.3	3696.7	4666.1	2323.9	3226.5	2775.2	3153.4
Manufactured Goods	7984.2	8459.5	12778.7	18508.0	27572.9	8221.9	15643.4	11932.6	15060.7
Difference (Terms-of-Trade Effects)	16871.9	22531.9	17873.8	12321.6	15106.6	19701.9	15097.7	17399.8	16941.2
of which: Pure Terms-of-Trade Effect	3115.9	9827.0	7681.9	3469.9	7505.0	6471.5	5575.9	6023.7	6319.9
Unbalanced Trade Effect	13756.0	12704.9	10191.9	8851.7	7601.6	13230.5	9521.8	11376.1	10621.2
Trend Value of Exports in "1972" Prices	31674.8	34938.9	38645.7	42860.6	47660.9	33306.9	40753.2	37030.0	39156.2
Hypothetical Exports in "1972" Prices	31208.2	31163.9	36343.7	37417.8	40719.3	31186.1	36880.8	34033.4	35370.6
Difference (Export Volume Effects of Changes in Foreign Demand)	466.6	3775.0	2302.0	5442.8	6941.6	2120.8	3872.4	2996.6	3785.6
of which: Traditional Primary Products	144.8	352.2	158.8	382.6	240.9	248.5	270.7	259.6	255.9
Non-traditional Primary Products	619.8	761.2	597.6	1017.4	1260.9	690.5	807.5	749.0	851.4
Fuels	29.5	261.4	237.2	337.7	491.3	145.5	287.5	216.5	271.4
Manufactured Goods	-327.5	2400.2	1308.4	3705.1	4948.5	1036.4	2506.8	1771.6	2406.9
of which: Growth Effects	821.1	3168.7	3429.1	4452.3	5836.6	1994.9	3940.7	2967.8	3541.6
Income Elasticity Effects	-1148.6	-768.5	-2120.7	-747.2	-888.1	-958.6	-1434.0	-1196.3	-1134.6
II. Policy Responses									
Actual Resource Gap in Current Prices	21962.0	20570.0	11861.0	5514.0	1261.0	21266.0	8687.5	14976.8	12233.6
Trend Value of Resource Gap, in "1972" Prices	2311.4	2447.2	3139.9	7260.9	5195.7	2379.3	5200.4	3789.9	4071.0
Difference (Additional Net External Financing)	19650.6	18122.8	8721.1	-1746.9	-3934.7	18886.7	3487.1	11186.9	8162.6
Actual Exports in "1972" Prices	29737.2	30643.5	35378.4	37596.9	42919.6	30190.4	36487.7	33339.0	35255.1
Hypothetical Exports, in "1972" Prices	31208.2	31163.9	36343.7	37417.8	40719.3	31186.1	36880.8	34033.4	35370.6
Difference (Increase in Export Market Shares)	-1471.0	-520.4	-965.3	179.1	2200.3	-995.7	-393.1	-694.4	-115.5
of which: Traditional Primary Products	-682.5	-704.1	-803.8	-400.6	-453.1	-693.3	-602.2	-647.8	-608.8
Non-traditional Primary Products	-103.9	200.6	312.2	659.5	1166.2	48.4	485.9	267.1	446.9
Fuels	-319.3	-159.9	-243.2	-79.9	216.4	-239.6	-161.6	-200.6	-117.2
Manufactured Goods	-365.3	143.0	-230.5	0.1	1270.8	-111.2	-115.2	-113.2	163.6
Hypothetical Imports, in "1972" Prices	48245.6	50556.0	54283.3	56268.0	61176.4	49400.8	55275.7	52338.2	54105.9
Actual Imports, in "1972" Prices	48816.3	44666.6	46255.6	45971.3	48924.0	46741.5	46113.5	46427.5	46926.8
Difference (Import Substitution)	-570.7	5889.4	8027.7	10296.7	12252.0	2659.4	9162.2	5910.8	7179.0
of which: Food	757.7	1381.5	1284.1	435.5	761.3	1069.6	859.8	964.7	924.0
Fuels	437.4	659.4	449.5	755.8	658.1	548.4	602.7	575.5	592.0
Other Primary Products	-108.2	977.2	934.2	676.8	1044.3	434.5	805.5	620.0	704.9
Capital Goods	-1553.6	-354.2	1292.8	2771.7	1140.1	-953.9	2032.3	539.2	659.4
Other Manufactures	-104.0	3225.5	4067.1	5656.9	8648.6	1560.8	4862.0	3211.4	4298.8
Trend Value of Imports in "1972" Prices	47975.2	53371.1	58675.6	65303.5	72706.6	50673.2	61989.6	56331.4	59606.4
Hypothetical Imports, in "1972" Prices	48245.6	50556.0	54283.3	56268.0	61176.4	49400.8	55275.7	52338.2	54105.9
Difference (Import Effects of Lower GNP Growth Rate)	-270.4	2815.1	4392.3	9035.5	11530.2	1272.4	6713.9	3993.2	5500.5
of which: Food	-26.9	235.7	418.9	792.8	973.7	104.4	605.9	355.1	478.8
Fuels	-22.9	236.6	423.8	807.0	1005.3	106.9	615.4	361.2	490.9
Other Primary Products	-37.1	290.2	524.5	1009.1	1255.8	126.6	766.8	446.7	608.5
Capital Goods	-75.9	763.0	1373.0	2625.4	3283.0	343.6	1999.2	1171.4	1593.7
Other Manufactures	-107.6	1289.6	1652.1	3801.2	5012.4	590.9	2726.6	1658.8	2329.5

Sources: See Annex C.

Appendix Table IV-1 (Cont'd)

	1974	1975	1976	1977	1978	1974-75	1976-77	1974-77	1974-78
	Relatively Industrialised Countries with Economies Based Predominantly on Agriculture								
I. External Shocks									
Effects of Increased Import Prices	8625.1	11181.8	11767.4	14967.0	18881.1	9903.5	13367.2	11635.4	13084.5
of which: Food	1703.9	2096.9	1465.7	1469.9	2037.7	1900.0	1467.8	1683.9	1754.6
Fuels	2102.7	2511.0	3070.4	3765.3	3972.9	2306.9	3417.9	2862.4	3084.5
Other Primary Products	691.0	601.2	676.7	1023.1	1137.2	646.1	849.9	748.0	825.8
Capital Goods	1301.2	2645.9	3352.2	4468.1	5805.6	1973.6	3910.2	2941.9	3514.6
Other Manufactures	2826.3	3327.7	3202.4	4240.6	5927.7	3077.0	3721.5	3399.3	3904.9
Effects of Increased Export Prices	7496.8	5931.7	7768.2	10797.5	13464.9	6714.3	9282.9	7998.6	9091.8
of which: Traditional Primary Products	4686.5	3222.6	3802.6	5515.4	6419.9	3954.6	4659.0	4306.8	4729.4
Non-traditional Primary Products	1456.1	1286.5	1764.5	2499.3	3263.8	1371.3	2131.9	1751.6	2054.0
Fuels	547.7	570.0	990.3	1115.4	1305.3	558.9	1052.9	805.9	905.7
Manufactured Goods	806.5	852.6	1211.8	1667.4	2475.9	829.6	1439.6	1134.6	1402.8
Difference (Terms-of-Trade Effects)	1128.3	5250.1	3999.2	4169.5	5416.2	3189.2	4084.4	3636.8	3992.7
of which: Pure Terms-of-Trade Effect	-1616.8	1632.3	974.5	-1125.4	-629.1	7.8	-75.5	-33.9	-152.9
Unbalanced Trade Effect	2745.1	3617.8	3024.7	5294.9	6045.3	3181.5	4159.8	3670.6	4145.6
Trend Value of Exports in "1972" Prices	9379.4	9946.4	10569.6	11256.0	12014.1	9662.9	10912.8	10287.9	10633.1
Hypothetical Exports in "1972" Prices	8929.6	8823.4	9770.5	9870.1	10258.1	8876.5	9820.3	9348.4	9530.3
Difference (Export Volume Effects of Changes in Foreign Demand)	449.8	1123.0	799.1	1385.9	1756.0	786.4	1092.5	939.5	1102.8
of which: Traditional Primary Products	339.9	685.6	514.9	771.7	935.6	512.8	643.3	578.1	649.5
Non-traditional Primary Products	164.5	202.0	158.6	270.0	334.6	183.3	214.3	198.8	225.9
Fuels	10.0	88.5	80.4	114.3	166.3	49.3	97.4	73.3	91.9
Manufactured Goods	-64.6	147.0	45.2	229.9	319.5	41.2	137.6	89.4	135.4
of which: Growth Effects	54.3	246.3	261.8	339.5	455.8	150.3	300.7	225.5	271.5
Income Elasticity Effects	-118.9	-99.3	-216.6	-109.6	-136.3	-109.1	-163.1	-136.1	-136.1
II. Policy Responses									
Actual Resource Gap in Current Prices	1831.0	2734.0	2127.0	5088.0	3922.0	2282.5	3607.5	2945.0	3140.4
Trend Value of Resource Gap, in "1972" Prices	-2007.8	-5476.4	-4283.4	-3553.5	-5845.6	-3742.1	-3918.5	-3830.3	-4233.3
Difference (Additional Net External Financing)	3838.8	8210.4	6410.4	8641.5	9767.6	6024.6	7526.0	6775.3	7373.7
Actual Exports in "1972" Prices	8508.2	8674.2	10099.8	9898.5	10862.1	8591.2	9999.2	9295.2	9608.6
Hypothetical Exports, in "1972" Prices	8929.6	8823.4	9770.5	9870.1	10258.1	8876.5	9820.3	9348.4	9530.3
Difference (Increase in Export Market Shares)	-421.4	-149.2	329.3	28.4	604.0	-285.3	178.9	-53.2	78.2
of which: Traditional Primary Products	-293.9	-92.4	287.0	264.7	207.6	-193.2	275.9	41.3	74.6
Non-traditional Primary Products	-28.6	-33.6	105.6	-62.6	403.1	-31.1	21.5	-4.8	76.8
Fuels	-179.7	-137.8	-64.8	-64.1	-1.1	-158.8	-64.5	-111.6	-89.5
Manufactured Goods	80.8	114.7	1.5	-109.6	-5.6	97.8	-54.1	21.9	16.4
Hypothetical Imports, in "1972" Prices	10812.8	11339.4	12163.4	12820.6	13484.6	11076.1	12492.0	11784.1	12124.2
Actual Imports, in "1972" Prices	12480.9	12823.2	13596.6	15318.0	15980.9	12652.1	14457.3	13554.7	14039.9
Difference (Import Substitution)	-1668.1	-1483.8	-1433.2	-2497.4	-2496.3	-1576.0	-1964.8	-1770.7	-1915.8
of which: Food	-444.9	-471.8	-415.7	-631.0	-886.9	-458.4	-523.4	-490.9	-570.1
Fuels	98.5	55.0	6.6	-60.8	-78.9	76.8	-27.1	24.9	4.1
Other Primary Products	-45.2	-19.2	66.2	-115.5	14.8	-32.2	-24.7	-28.4	-19.8
Capital Goods	-929.1	-1036.2	-1036.2	-1217.9	-1211.1	-982.7	-1127.1	-1054.9	-1086.1
Other Manufactures	-347.4	-11.6	-54.1	-472.2	-334.2	-179.5	-263.2	-221.3	-243.9
Trend Value of Imports in "1972" Prices	10641.6	11135.0	11655.2	12203.5	12781.5	10888.3	11929.4	11408.8	11683.4
Hypothetical Imports, in "1972" Prices	10812.8	11339.4	12163.4	12820.6	13484.6	11076.1	12492.0	11784.1	12124.2
Difference (Import Effects of Lower GNP Growth Rate)	-171.2	-204.4	-508.2	-617.1	-703.1	-187.8	-562.7	-375.2	-440.8
of which: Food	-0.7	-1.0	-1.4	-1.7	-2.1	-0.9	-1.6	-1.2	-1.4
Fuels	-7.9	-8.4	-24.4	-28.4	-30.8	-8.2	-26.4	-17.3	-20.0
Other Primary Products	-19.8	-24.4	-59.1	-72.8	-84.2	-22.1	-66.0	-44.0	-52.1
Capital Goods	-56.0	-64.6	-166.8	-200.1	-225.7	-60.3	-183.5	-121.9	-142.6
Other Manufactures	-86.8	-106.0	-256.5	-314.1	-360.3	-96.3	-285.2	-190.8	-224.7

Sources: See Annex C.

Appendix Table IV-1 (Cont'd)

	1974	1975	1976	1977	1978	1974-75	1976-77	1974-77	1974-78
	Relatively Industrialised Countries with Economies Based Predominantly on Mineral Production								
I. External Shocks									
Effects of Increased Import Prices	2299.5	3100.6	2945.8	3429.3	4222.5	2700.1	3187.6	2943.8	3199.5
of which: Food	640.8	653.4	493.7	406.3	653.9	647.1	450.0	548.6	569.6
Fuels	529.1	699.7	824.6	927.3	865.5	614.4	876.0	745.2	769.2
Other Primary Products	151.3	244.7	200.8	289.7	349.1	198.0	245.3	221.6	247.1
Capital Goods	315.4	659.5	710.0	839.7	1061.2	487.5	774.9	631.2	717.2
Other Manufactures	662.9	843.3	716.7	966.3	1292.8	753.1	841.5	797.3	896.4
Effects of Increased Export Prices	2353.2	1495.5	1595.8	1971.1	2487.3	1924.4	1783.5	1853.9	1980.6
of which: Traditional Primary Products	1400.6	546.6	584.2	553.9	619.2	973.6	569.1	771.3	740.9
Non-traditional Primary Products	428.5	374.7	425.7	650.4	921.5	401.6	538.1	469.8	560.2
Fuels	278.2	306.9	294.9	362.2	400.9	292.6	328.6	310.6	328.6
Manufactured Goods	245.9	267.3	291.0	404.6	545.7	256.6	347.8	302.2	350.9
Difference (Terms-of-Trade Effects)	-53.7	1605.1	1350.0	1458.2	1735.2	775.7	1404.1	1089.9	1218.9
of which: Pure Terms-of-Trade Effect	-4.7	1282.1	1228.1	1322.1	1787.7	638.7	1275.1	956.9	1123.1
Unbalanced Trade Effect	-49.0	323.0	121.9	136.1	-52.5	137.0	129.0	133.0	95.9
Trend Value of Exports in "1972" Prices	2969.1	3133.5	3292.2	3508.4	3699.1	3051.3	3400.3	3225.8	3320.5
Hypothetical Exports in "1972" Prices	2940.5	2776.9	3002.6	3058.5	3141.3	2858.7	3030.6	2944.6	2984.0
Difference (Export Volume Effects of Changes in Foreign Demand)	28.6	356.6	289.6	449.9	557.8	192.6	369.8	281.2	336.5
of which: Traditional Primary Products	-12.3	213.0	190.2	229.3	275.3	100.4	209.8	155.1	179.1
Non-traditional Primary Products	43.9	54.0	42.4	92.6	110.6	49.0	67.5	58.3	68.7
Fuels	3.4	29.3	26.7	37.9	55.1	16.4	32.3	24.4	30.5
Manufactured Goods	-6.4	60.3	30.3	90.1	116.8	27.0	60.2	43.6	58.2
of which: Growth Effects	20.9	78.0	84.3	109.2	141.9	49.5	96.8	73.1	86.9
Income Elasticity Effects	-27.3	-17.7	-54.0	-19.1	-25.1	-22.5	-36.6	-29.5	-28.6
II. Policy Responses									
Actual Resource Gap in Current Prices	-305.1	1558.6	261.0	605.4	37.9	626.8	433.2	530.0	431.6
Trend Value of Resource Gap, in "1972" Prices	32.2	-255.6	-1075.4	-781.8	-1664.6	-111.7	-928.6	-520.2	-749.0
Difference (Additional Net External Financing)	-337.3	1814.2	1336.4	1387.2	1702.5	738.5	1361.8	1050.2	1180.6
Actual Exports in "1972" Prices	3274.8	3165.5	3172.2	3484.9	3680.7	3220.2	3328.6	3274.4	3355.6
Hypothetical Exports, in "1972" Prices	2940.5	2776.9	3002.6	3058.5	3141.3	2858.7	3030.6	2944.6	2984.0
Difference (Increase in Export Market Shares)	334.3	388.6	169.6	426.4	539.4	361.5	298.0	329.8	371.7
of which: Traditional Primary Products	171.2	115.5	219.4	380.8	351.5	143.4	300.1	221.7	247.7
Non-traditional Primary Products	52.8	124.1	-0.5	99.6	263.2	88.5	49.6	69.0	107.8
Fuels	-25.1	-6.7	-31.6	-23.3	-8.9	-15.9	-27.5	-21.7	-19.1
Manufactured Goods	135.4	155.7	-17.7	-30.7	-66.4	145.6	-24.2	60.7	35.3
Hypothetical Imports, in "1972" Prices	3179.6	3152.9	3228.6	3282.2	3307.6	3166.3	3255.4	3210.9	3230.2
Actual Imports, in "1972" Prices	3206.5	3533.4	3309.2	3467.7	3635.5	3370.0	3388.5	3379.2	3430.5
Difference (Import Substitution)	-26.9	-380.5	-80.6	-185.5	-327.9	-203.7	-133.1	-168.4	-200.3
of which: Food	-26.9	73.0	64.5	124.3	-39.3	23.1	94.4	58.8	39.1
Fuels	49.9	4.1	-3.5	-0.9	21.0	27.0	-2.2	12.4	14.1
Other Primary Products	-16.7	-197.8	-92.6	-147.2	-159.4	-107.3	-119.9	-113.6	-122.7
Capital Goods	-126.8	-231.6	-105.8	-56.4	-67.0	-179.2	-81.1	-130.2	-117.5
Other Manufactures	93.6	-28.2	56.8	-105.3	-83.2	32.7	-24.3	4.2	-13.3
Trend Value of Imports in "1972" Prices	3184.4	3292.3	3442.8	3562.2	3686.6	3238.4	3502.5	3370.5	3433.7
Hypothetical Imports, in "1972" Prices	3179.6	3152.9	3228.6	3282.2	3307.6	3166.3	3255.4	3210.9	3230.2
Difference (Import Effects of Lower GNP Growth Rate)	4.8	139.4	214.2	280.0	379.0	72.1	247.1	159.6	203.5
of which: Food	0.4	33.5	42.7	58.2	81.6	17.0	50.5	33.7	43.3
Fuels	-0.3	17.0	21.9	30.3	43.0	8.4	26.1	17.3	22.4
Other Primary Products	4.7	10.9	12.7	15.4	19.6	7.8	14.1	11.0	12.7
Capital Goods	0.3	10.8	13.3	18.3	25.6	5.6	15.8	10.7	13.7
Other Manufactures	-0.3	67.2	123.6	157.8	209.2	33.3	140.6	86.9	111.4

Sources: See Annex C.

Appendix Table IV-1 (Cont'd)

	1974	1975	1976	1977	1978	1974-75	1976-77	1974-77	1974-78
	Less Industrialised Countries with Economies Based Predominantly on Agriculture								
I. External Shocks									
Effects of Increased Import Prices	2290.0	2761.8	2732.3	3792.6	5195.1	2525.9	3262.5	2894.2	3354.4
of which: Food	441.8	502.6	342.6	422.5	597.0	472.2	382.6	427.4	461.3
Fuels	639.8	707.9	699.6	870.9	1160.9	673.6	785.8	729.4	815.7
Other Primary Products	78.4	62.1	91.6	125.7	113.5	70.3	108.7	89.5	94.3
Capital Goods	268.5	541.2	670.9	1073.6	1652.4	404.9	872.3	638.6	841.3
Other Manufactures	862.0	948.0	927.6	1299.9	1671.3	905.0	1113.8	1009.4	1141.8
Effects of Increased Export Prices	1846.6	1897.8	2844.8	4974.1	4966.2	1872.2	3909.5	2890.8	3305.9
of which: Traditional Primary Products	943.3	1012.2	1873.7	3722.4	3522.1	977.8	2798.1	1887.9	2214.7
Non-traditional Primary Products	593.6	562.5	571.5	726.9	785.2	578.1	649.2	613.7	647.9
Fuels	168.6	177.8	213.5	255.5	297.0	173.2	234.5	203.9	222.5
Manufactured Goods	141.1	145.3	186.1	269.3	361.9	143.2	227.7	185.5	220.7
Difference (Terms-of-Trade Effects)	443.4	864.0	-112.5	-1181.5	228.9	653.7	-647.0	3.4	48.5
of which: Pure Terms-of-Trade Effect	313.6	850.5	-209.8	-2314.3	-1598.7	582.1	-1262.1	-340.0	-591.7
Unbalanced Trade Effect	129.8	13.5	97.3	1132.8	1827.6	71.7	615.1	343.4	640.2
Trend Value of Exports in "1972" Prices	209.0	3362.3	3528.3	3708.1	3903.2	3285.7	3618.2	3452.0	3542.2
Hypothetical Exports in "1972" Prices	025.1	3020.6	3269.3	3147.7	3328.8	3022.9	3208.5	3115.7	3158.3
Difference (Export Volume Effects of Changes in Foreign Demand)	183.9	341.7	259.0	560.4	574.4	262.8	409.7	336.3	383.9
of which: Traditional Primary Products	141.2	244.9	202.1	430.3	400.3	193.1	316.2	254.7	283.8
Non-traditional Primary Products	69.5	85.4	67.0	114.1	141.4	77.5	90.6	84.0	95.5
Fuels	1.9	16.8	15.3	21.7	31.6	9.4	18.5	14.0	17.5
Manufactured Goods	-28.7	-5.4	-25.4	-5.7	1.1	-17.1	-15.6	-16.3	-12.8
of which: Growth Effects	0.7	27.4	26.4	34.4	52.2	14.1	30.4	22.3	28.2
Income Elasticity Effects	-29.4	-32.8	-51.8	-40.1	-51.1	-31.1	-46.0	-38.5	-41.0
II. Policy Responses									
Actual Resource Gap in Current Prices	698.0	991.0	133.0	7.0	1017.0	845.0	70.0	457.5	569.2
Trend Value of Resource Gap, in "1972" Prices	64.9	21.6	-48.4	-294.2	-1143.0	43.3	-171.3	-64.0	-279.8
Difference (Additional Net External Financing)	633.1	969.4	181.4	301.2	2160.0	801.3	241.3	521.3	849.0
Actual Exports in "1972" Prices	956.4	3065.2	3100.2	2823.9	2832.8	3010.8	2962.4	2986.4	2955.7
Hypothetical Exports, in "1972" Prices	025.1	3020.6	3269.3	3147.7	3328.8	3022.9	3208.5	3115.7	3158.3
Difference (Increase in Export Market Shares)	-68.7	44.6	-169.1	-323.8	-496.0	-12.1	-246.5	-129.3	-202.6
of which: Traditional Primary Products	26.5	28.1	96.8	30.5	-105.2	27.3	63.7	45.5	15.3
Non-traditional Primary Products	-37.8	77.2	-154.8	-231.6	-245.2	19.7	-193.2	-86.8	-118.4
Fuels	-11.1	-3.1	-4.5	-0.2	13.2	-7.1	-2.4	-4.7	-1.1
Manufactured Goods	-46.3	-57.6	-106.6	-122.5	-158.8	-52.0	-114.6	-83.3	-98.4
Hypothetical Imports, in "1972" Prices	3159.6	3193.2	3244.6	3315.0	3414.0	3176.4	3279.8	3228.1	3265.3
Actual Imports, in "1972" Prices	3134.0	3080.2	3214.7	4026.4	4369.9	3107.1	3620.6	3363.8	3565.0
Difference (Import Substitution)	25.6	113.0	29.9	-711.4	-955.9	69.3	-340.8	-135.7	-299.7
of which: Food	85.9	115.6	141.7	-11.5	-93.6	100.8	65.1	83.0	47.6
Fuels	-19.4	-21.3	4.5	-21.7	-98.5	-20.4	-8.6	-14.5	-31.3
Other Primary Products	-7.8	-8.9	-39.0	-57.4	-18.4	-8.4	-48.2	-28.3	-26.3
Capital Goods	-32.8	-73.5	-82.0	-368.2	-641.5	-53.2	-230.1	-141.7	-241.6
Other Manufactures	-0.3	101.1	14.7	-252.6	-103.9	50.4	-119.0	-34.3	-48.2
Trend Value of Imports in "1972" Prices	3196.9	3271.9	3348.9	3427.9	3509.2	3234.4	3388.4	3311.4	3351.0
Hypothetical Imports, in "1972" Prices	3159.6	3193.2	3244.6	3315.0	3414.0	3176.4	3279.8	3228.1	3265.3
Difference (Import Effects of Lower GNP Growth Rate)	37.3	78.7	104.3	112.9	95.2	58.0	108.6	83.3	85.7
of which: Food	-0.2	0.6	0.6	-0.2	-2.0	0.2	0.2	0.2	-0.2
Fuels	3.3	6.0	9.5	12.7	12.8	4.7	11.1	7.9	8.9
Other Primary Products	-1.0	-0.9	-1.3	-2.3	-4.1	-1.0	-1.8	-1.4	-1.9
Capital Goods	22.5	41.3	54.9	63.4	64.6	31.9	59.2	45.5	49.3
Other Manufactures	12.7	31.7	40.6	39.3	23.9	22.2	39.9	31.1	29.6

Sources: See Annex C.

Appendix Table IV-1 (Cont'd)

	1974	1975	1976	1977	1978	1974-75	1976-77	1974-77	1974-78
	Less Industrialised Countries with Economies Based Predominatly on Mineral Production								
I. External Shocks									
Effects of Increased Import Prices	1373.1	1727.1	1485.1	1728.3	..	1550.1	1606.7	1578.4	..
of which: Food	270.2	282.4	215.6	221.9	..	276.3	218.8	247.5	..
Fuels	257.2	328.4	317.2	350.4	..	292.8	333.8	313.3	..
Other Primary Products	21.5	20.5	19.3	24.6	..	21.0	22.0	21.5	..
Capital Goods	212.6	427.3	413.4	495.1	..	320.0	454.3	387.1	..
Other Manufactures	611.6	668.5	519.6	636.3	..	640.1	578.0	609.0	..
Effects of Increased Export Prices	1944.1	662.9	1185.1	1584.9	..	1303.5	1385.0	1344.3	..
of which: Traditional Primary Products	1167.6	129.8	591.7	858.2	..	648.7	725.0	686.8	..
Non-traditional Primary Products	573.2	363.6	387.7	514.8	..	468.4	451.3	459.8	..
Fuels	149.5	123.8	135.9	113.2	..	136.7	124.6	130.5	
Manufactured Goods	53.8	45.7	69.8	98.7	..	49.8	84.3	67.0	..
Difference (Terms-of-Trade Effects)	-571.0	1064.2	300.0	143.4	..	246.6	221.7	234.2	..
of which: Pure Terms-of-Trade Effect	-166.6	1488.2	980.5	617.2	..	660.8	798.9	729.8	..
Unbalanced Trade Effect	-404.4	-424.0	-680.5	-473.8	..	-414.2	-577.2	-495.7	..
									..
									..
									..
Trend Value of Exports in "1972" Prices	2946.4	3090.6	3243.5	3364.2	..	3018.5	3303.9	3161.2	...
Hypothetical Exports in "1972" Prices	2930.9	2772.6	2953.2	2952.2	..	2851.8	2952.7	2902.3	..
Difference (Export Volume Effects of Changes in Foreign Demand)	15.5	318.0	290.3	412.0	..	166.8	351.2	259.0	..
of which: Traditional Primary Products	-44.6	188.0	199.4	235.9	..	71.7	217.7	144.7	..
Non-traditional Primary Products	54.9	67.5	53.0	90.1	..	61.2	71.6	66.4	..
Fuels	1.6	14.0	12.7	18.1	..	7.8	15.4	11.6	..
Manufactured Goods	3.6	48.5	25.2	67.9	..	26.1	46.6	36.3	..
of which: Growth Effects	16.8	53.4	58.4	75.0	..	35.1	66.7	50.9	..
Income Elasticity Effects	-13.2	-4.9	-33.2	-7.1	..	-9.1	-20.2	-14.6	..
II. Policy Responses									
Actual Resource Gap in Current Prices	-277.2	618.6	665.5	159.4	..	170.7	412.5	291.6	..
Trend Value of Resource Gap, in "1972" Prices	533.6	-321.5	811.2	196.2	..	106.1	503.7	304.9	..
Difference (Additional Net External Financing)	-810.8	940.1	-145.7	-36.8	..	64.7	-91.3	-13.3	..
Actual Exports in "1972" Prices	2824.9	2638.1	2654.9	2409.1	..	2731.5	2532.0	2631.8	..
Hypothetical Exports, in "1972" Prices	2930.9	2772.6	2953.2	2952.2	..	2851.8	2952.7	2902.3	...
Difference (Increase in Export Market Shares)	-106.0	-134.5	-298.3	-543.1	..	-120.3	-420.7	-270.5	..
of which: Traditional Primary Products	-144.4	-22.1	53.8	-242.6	..	-83.3	-94.4	-88.9	..
Non-traditional Primary Products	131.0	-6.3	-196.9	-134.8	..	62.4	-165.9	-51.7	..
Fuels	-6.3	-11.0	-16.9	-27.7	..	-8.7	-22.3	-15.5	..
Manufactured Goods	-86.3	-95.1	-138.3	-138.0	..	-90.7	-138.2	-114.4	..
Hypothetical Imports, in "1972" Prices	2448.7	2418.0	2439.1	2463.8	..	2433.4	2451.5	2442.4	..
Actual Imports, in "1972" Prices	2181.9	2117.9	1820.9	1890.7	..	2149.9	1855.8	2002.9	..
Difference (Import Substitution)	266.8	300.1	618.2	573.1	..	283.5	595.7	439.6	..
of which: Food	108.5	142.2	131.5	96.7	..	125.4	114.1	119.8	..
Fuels	43.0	25.2	40.0	41.3	..	34.1	40.7	37.4	..
Other Primary Products	11.4	7.1	12.7	11.2	..	9.3	12.0	10.6	..
Capital Goods	142.5	90.6	247.7	278.0	..	116.6	262.9	189.7	..
Other Manufactures	-38.6	35.0	186.3	145.9	..	-1.8	166.1	82.2	..
Trend Value of Imports in "1972" Prices	2543.2	2694.5	2855.2	3026.0	...	2618.9	2940.6	2779.8	..
Hypothetical Imports, in "1972" Prices	2448.7	2418.0	2439.1	2463.8	..	2433.4	2451.5	2442.4	..
Difference (Import Effects of Lower GNP Growth Rate)	94.5	276.5	416.1	562.2	..	185.5	489.2	337.3	..
of which: Food	17.6	50.4	76.0	102.8	..	34.0	89.4	61.7	..
Fuels	3.6	11.3	16.9	22.7	..	7.5	19.8	13.7	..
Other Primary Products	0.7	2.3	3.3	4.4	..	1.5	3.9	2.7	..
Capital Goods	42.3	125.1	189.6	258.0	..	83.7	223.8	153.8	..
Other Manufactures	30.3	87.4	130.3	174.3	..	58.9	152.3	105.6	..

Sources: See Annex C.

Appendix Table IV-1 (Cont'd)

	1974	1975	1976	1977	1978	1974-75	1976-77	1974-77	1974-78
	Least Developed Countries								
I. External Shocks									
Effects of Increased Import Prices	999.8	1305.7	1204.3	1468.3	2064.3	1152.8	1336.3	1244.6	1408.5
of which: Food	241.4	250.8	191.6	200.1	258.4	246.1	195.9	221.0	228.5
Fuels	235.2	222.0	227.4	280.8	323.6	228.6	254.1	241.4	257.8
Other Primary Products	34.1	28.5	29.4	38.1	54.2	31.3	33.8	32.5	36.9
Capital Goods	138.5	312.0	333.9	453.1	597.6	225.3	393.5	309.4	367.0
Other Manufactures	350.6	492.4	422.0	496.2	830.5	421.5	459.1	440.3	518.3
Effects of Increased Export Prices	634.9	561.5	930.1	1616.4	1248.5	598.2	1273.3	935.7	998.3
of which: Traditional Primary Products	447.2	372.6	705.2	1380.8	1003.7	409.9	1043.0	726.5	781.9
Non-traditional Primary Products	131.0	126.5	167.5	165.7	168.5	128.8	166.6	147.7	151.8
Fuels	30.3	33.3	32.8	31.5	31.6	31.8	32.2	32.0	31.9
Manufactured Goods	26.4	29.1	24.6	38.4	44.7	27.8	31.5	29.7	32.6
Difference (Terms-of-Trade Effects)	364.9	744.2	274.2	-148.1	815.8	554.6	63.1	308.8	410.2
of which: Pure Terms-of-Trade Effect	50.9	315.1	-2.0	-720.9	-263.1	183.0	-361.5	-89.2	-124.0
Unbalanced Trade Effect	314.0	429.1	276.2	572.8	1078.9	371.6	424.5	398.0	534.2
Trend Value of Exports in "1972" Prices	1445.0	1479.2	1545.4	1601.0	1660.7	1462.1	1573.2	1517.7	1546.3
Hypothetical Exports in "1972" Prices	1344.2	1362.8	1440.9	1355.1	1466.0	1353.5	1398.0	1375.8	1393.8
Difference (Export Volume Effects of Changes in Foreign Demand)	100.8	116.4	104.6	245.9	194.7	108.6	175.2	141.9	152.5
of which: Traditional Primary Products	74.9	65.1	68.0	176.7	106.9	70.0	122.4	96.2	98.3
Non-traditional Primary Products	27.3	33.6	26.4	44.9	55.6	30.5	35.7	33.1	37.6
Fuels	0.7	6.8	6.2	8.8	12.7	3.8	7.5	5.7	7.0
Manufactured Goods	-2.1	10.9	3.9	15.5	19.5	4.4	9.7	7.1	9.5
of which: Growth Effects	3.9	15.2	16.1	20.8	27.0	9.6	18.5	14.0	16.6
Income Elasticity Effects	-6.0	-4.3	-12.2	-5.3	-7.5	-5.2	-8.8	-7.0	-7.1
II. Policy Responses									
Actual Resource Gap in Current Prices	796.0	976.0	263.0	398.0	1120.0	886.0	330.5	608.3	710.6
Trend Value of Resource Gap, in "1972" Prices	192.1	-37.9	-88.4	209.7	-334.4	77.1	60.7	68.9	-11.8
Difference (Additional Net External Financing)	603.9	1013.9	351.4	188.3	1454.4	808.9	269.9	539.4	722.4
Actual Exports in "1972" Prices	994.1	1073.5	1158.9	985.6	875.5	1033.8	1072.3	1053.0	1017.5
Hypothetical Exports, in "1972" Prices	1344.2	1362.8	1440.9	1355.1	1466.0	1353.5	1398.0	1375.8	1393.8
Difference (Increase in Export Market Shares)	-350.1	-289.3	-282.0	-369.5	-590.5	-319.7	-325.8	-322.7	-376.3
of which: Traditional Primary Products	-155.8	-125.7	-59.8	-88.3	-276.0	-140.8	-74.1	-107.4	-141.1
Non-traditional Primary Products	-150.8	-129.9	-142.7	-201.8	-217.2	-140.4	-172.3	-156.3	-168.5
Fuels	-17.8	-13.9	-18.0	-19.5	-18.6	-15.9	-18.8	-17.3	-17.6
Manufactured Goods	-25.7	-19.8	-61.5	-59.9	-78.7	-22.8	-60.7	-41.70	-49.1
Hypothetical Imports, in "1972" Prices	1677.8	1708.0	1748.3	1836.0	1823.0	1692.9	1792.2	1742.5	1758.6
Actual Imports, in "1972" Prices	1449.2	1599.3	1503.7	1615.7	1833.7	1524.3	1559.7	1542.0	1600.3
Difference (Import Substitution)	228.6	108.7	244.6	220.3	-10.7	168.7	232.5	200.6	158.3
of which: Food	1.8	43.3	37.7	14.7	-1.9	22.6	26.2	24.4	19.1
Fuels	32.7	48.8	59.5	63.1	49.4	40.8	61.3	51.5	50.7
Other Primary Products	4.5	4.6	10.2	9.6	-1.3	4.6	9.9	7.2	5.5
Capital Goods	10.3	-65.9	6.0	-16.9	-51.8	-27.8	-5.5	-16.6	-23.7
Other Manufactures	179.3	77.9	131.2	149.8	-5.1	128.6	140.5	134.6	106.6
Trend Value of Imports in "1972" Prices	1661.1	1735.3	1813.0	1894.7	1980.3	1698.2	1853.9	1776.0	1816.9
Hypothetical Imports, in "1972" Prices	1677.8	1708.0	1748.3	1836.0	1823.0	1692.9	1792.2	1742.5	1758.6
Difference (Import Effects of Lower GNP Growth Rate)	-16.7	27.3	64.7	58.7	157.3	5.3	61.7	33.5	58.3
of which: Food	-3.2	4.5	11.0	9.7	27.3	0.7	10.4	5.5	9.9
Fuels	-0.4	6.4	12.7	13.6	29.3	3.0	13.2	8.1	12.3
Other Primary Products	-0.8	0.7	1.8	1.5	4.7	-0.1	1.7	0.8	1.6
Capital Goods	-5.8	7.2	18.1	15.7	45.0	0.7	16.9	8.8	16.0
Other Manufactures	-6.5	8.5	21.1	18.2	51.0	1.0	19.7	10.3	18.5

Sources: See Annex C.

Appendix Table IV-1 (Cont'd)

	1974	1975	1976	1977	1978	1974-75	1976-77	1974-77	1974-78
	South Asian Countries								
I. External Shocks									
Effects of Increased Import Prices	3670.0	4958.8	4275.8	5206.9	7058.5	4314.4	4741.4	4527.9	5034.0
of which: Food	945.3	1434.0	1065.4	696.8	1240.6	1189.7	881.1	1035.4	1076.4
Fuels	1289.9	1315.3	1344.6	1607.1	1973.3	1302.6	1475.9	1389.2	1506.0
Other Primary Products	286.5	239.4	266.5	533.4	576.9	263.0	400.0	331.5	380.5
Capital Goods	298.4	569.6	691.2	919.0	1315.3	434.0	805.1	619.6	758.7
Other Manufactures	849.9	1400.5	908.1	1450.6	1952.4	1125.2	1179.4	1152.3	1312.3
Effects of Increased Export Prices	1822.8	1937.0	2684.7	3838.1	4453.1	1879.9	3261.4	2570.7	2947.1
of which: Traditional Primary Products	360.7	357.8	461.3	937.5	901.2	359.3	699.4	529.3	603.7
Non-traditional Primary Products	683.9	808.0	1039.4	1224.9	1428.7	746.0	1132.2	939.1	1037.0
Fuels	37.6	37.6	46.7	70.5	72.7	37.6	58.6	48.1	53.0
Manufactured Goods	740.6	733.6	1137.3	1605.2	2050.5	737.1	1371.3	1054.2	1253.4
Difference (Terms-of-Trade Effects)	1847.2	3021.8	1591.1	1368.8	2605.4	2434.5	1480.0	1957.2	2086.9
of which: Pure Terms-of-Trade Effect	1218.1	1894.1	1517.3	471.7	799.4	1556.1	994.5	1275.3	1180.1
Unbalanced Trade Effect	629.1	1127.7	73.8	897.1	1806.0	878.4	485.5	681.9	906.7
Trend Value of Exports in "1972" Prices	4051.7	4460.8	4922.9	5457.3	6052.5	4256.3	5190.1	4723.2	4989.0
Hypothetical Exports in "1972" Prices	3976.2	3952.9	4547.8	4779.4	5106.3	3964.6	4663.6	4314.1	4472.5
Difference (Export Volume Effects of Changes in Foreign Demand)	75.5	507.9	375.1	677.9	946.2	291.7	526.5	409.1	516.5
of which: Traditional Primary Products	67.0	186.1	100.3	133.8	148.6	126.6	117.1	121.8	127.2
Non-traditional Primary Products	55.4	68.3	53.4	91.2	113.6	61.9	72.3	67.1	76.4
Fuels	0.9	8.3	7.5	10.6	15.4	4.6	9.1	6.8	8.5
Manufactured Goods	-47.8	245.2	213.9	442.3	668.6	98.7	328.1	213.4	304.4
of which: Growth Effects	75.1	327.8	358.4	473.4	641.8	201.5	415.9	308.7	375.3
Income Elasticity Effects	-122.9	-82.6	-144.5	-31.1	26.8	-102.8	-87.8	-95.3	-70.9
II. Policy Responses									
Actual Resource Gap in Current Prices	2018.0	1856.0	-404.0	-110.0	126.0	1937.0	-257.0	840.0	697.2
Trend Value of Resource Gap, in "1972" Prices	-954.1	-3182.5	-3497.0	-4381.6	-6621.3	-2068.3	-3939.3	-3003.8	-3727.3
Difference (Additional Net External Financing)	2972.1	5038.5	3093.0	4271.6	6747.3	4005.3	3682.3	3843.8	4424.5
Actual Exports in "1972" Prices	3559.2	3848.0	4434.3	4204.9	4238.9	3703.6	4319.6	4011.6	4057.1
Hypothetical Exports, in "1972" Prices	3976.2	3952.9	4547.8	4779.4	5106.3	3964.6	4663.6	4314.1	4472.5
Difference (Increase in Export Market Shares)	-417.0	-104.9	-113.5	-574.5	-867.4	-261.0	-344.0	-302.5	-415.5
of which: Traditional Primary Products	-7.4	94.5	133.5	11.0	-90.1	43.5	72.3	57.9	28.3
Non-traditional Primary Products	268.1	609.3	587.5	375.2	438.8	438.7	481.4	460.0	455.8
Fuels	-21.4	-17.9	-19.9	-15.1	-13.3	-19.7	-17.5	-18.6	-17.5
Manufactured Goods	-656.3	-790.8	-814.6	-945.6	-1202.8	-723.6	-880.1	-801.8	-882.0
Hypothetical Imports, in "1972" Prices	3672.1	3481.3	3438.4	3324.2	3247.0	3576.7	3381.3	3479.0	3432.6
Actual Imports, in "1972" Prices	4295.0	4980.2	4512.2	5080.1	5696.5	4637.6	4796.2	4716.9	4912.8
Difference (Import Substitution)	-622.9	-1498.9	-1073.8	-1755.9	-2449.5	-1060.9	-1414.9	-1237.9	-1480.2
of which: Food	101.0	-141.4	-176.4	171.8	-245.1	-20.2	-2.3	-11.3	-58.0
Fuels	9.0	86.6	133.3	141.8	78.9	47.8	137.6	92.7	89.9
Other Primary Products	136.2	116.4	122.6	-148.3	-103.7	126.3	-12.9	56.7	24.6
Capital Goods	-215.8	-361.0	-410.0	-583.6	-815.8	-288.4	-496.8	-392.6	-477.2
Other Manufactures	-653.3	-1199.5	-743.3	-1337.6	-1363.8	-926.4	-1040.5	-983.4	-1059.5
Trend Value of Imports in "1972" Prices	3662.6	3576.3	3498.9	3429.7	3368.2	3619.5	3464.3	3541.9	3507.2
Hypothetical Imports, in "1972" Prices	3672.1	3481.3	3438.4	3324.2	3247.0	3576.7	3381.3	3479.0	3432.6
Difference (Import Effects of Lower GNP Growth Rate)	-9.5	95.0	60.5	105.5	121.2	42.8	83.0	62.9	74.5
of which: Food	0.4	-3.4	-2.2	-4.9	-6.7	-1.5	-3.6	-2.5	-3.4
Fuels	2.0	-22.7	-15.3	-35.0	-50.4	-10.4	-25.2	-17.8	-24.3
Other Primary Products	-0.2	1.7	1.1	2.4	3.2	0.8	1.8	1.3	1.6
Capital Goods	-7.2	72.5	46.5	84.9	102.4	32.7	65.7	49.2	59.8
Other Manufactures	-4.5	46.9	30.4	58.1	72.7	21.2	44.3	32.7	40.7

Sources: See Annex C.

Appendix Table IV-2

Trade Effects of External Shocks and of Policy Responses to these Shocks : Merchandise Trade (1974-1977 Average)

	Newly Industrializing Countries	Relatively Industrialized Agricultural Countries	Relatively Industrialized Mineral-Producing Countries	Less Industrialized Agricultural Countries	Less Industrialized Mineral-Producing Countries	Least Developed Countries	South Asian Countries
EXPORTS							
Traditional Primary Products							
Hypothetical/Trend	94.8	89,6	92.1	87.4	93.0	90.4	88.9
Actual/Hypothetical	86.3	100.8	112.3	102.6	95.4	88.2	105.9
Fuels							
Hypothetical/Trend	83.0	83.0	83.0	83.0	83.1	83.0	83.1
Actual/Hypothetical	81.1	68.9	81.8	93.1	72.9	36.9	44.3
Non-traditional Primary Products							
Hypothetical/Trend	91.2	91.2	90.5	91.2	91.2	91.3	91.3
Actual/Hypothetical	103.4	99.8	112.5	90.1	92.5	54.7	165.6
Manufacturing Goods (a)							
Hypothetical/Trend	92.0 (88.0)	92.1	91.6	104.3	86.4	93.1	92.4
Actual/Hypothetical	99.5 (119.1)	101.1	112.8	79.2	50.4	55.8	69.2
Total							
Hypothetical/Trend	91.9	90.0	91.3	90.3	91.8	90.7	91.3
Actual/Hypothetical	98.0	99.4	111.2	95.9	90.7	76.5	93.0
IMPORTS							
Food							
Hypothetical/Trend	94.5	100.1	95.1	100.0	86.4	98.0	100.2
Actual/Hypothetical	84.1	136.6	91.0	85.0	69.4	90.9	101.0
Fuels							
Hypothetical/Trend	93.3	101.9	93.6	96.6	91.1	94.2	103.3
Actual/Hypothetical	88.5	97.4	95.1	106.5	73.3	60.8	83.1
Other Primary Products							
Hypothetical/Trend	93.4	104.5	94.7	101.4	93.9	98.5	99.8
Actual/Hypothetical	90.2	102.8	157.8	128.0	74.3	86.6	89.2
Capital Goods							
Hypothetical/Trend	92.9	103.2	98.9	95.3	85.0	98.3	93.1
Actual/Hypothetical	96.5	127.1	113.5	115.5	78.3	103.3	159.2
Other Manufactures							
Hypothetical/Trend	92.2	104.3	92.9	97.9	90.4	98.7	95.2
Actual/Hypothetical	83.5	104.8	99.6	102.4	91.8	82.9	252.9
Total							
Hypothetical/Trend	92.9	103.3	95.3	97.5	87.9	98.1	98.2
Actual/Hypothetical	88.7	115.0	105.2	104.2	82.0	88.5	135.6

List of Sources

TRADE STATISTICS

EXPORTS AND IMPORTS

Total : **International Monetary Fund**: International Financial Statistics, various issues.

Commodities : **Food and Agricultural Organization of the United Nations**: Trade Yearbook, various issues; Yearbook of Forestry Products, various issues; Yearbook of Fishery Statistics, various issues; Fertilizer Yearbook, various issues. **United Nations**: Yearbook of International Trade Statistics, various issues. **International Monetary Fund**: International Financial Statistics, various issues; Balance of Payments Yearbook, various issues. **Statistical Office of General Agreement on Tariffs and Trade**, (Geneva). **Statistical Office of the United Nations**, (New York). **World Bank**: Country Economic Memoranda; Price Prospects for Major Primary Commodities, various issues; World Development Report, 1978, 1979, 1980. **MINEMET** Yearbook, 1978. **Organisation for Economic Co-operation and Development**: Statistics of Foreign Trade, various issues. **Reserve Bank of India Bulletin**, various issues.

UNIT VALUE INDICES

United Nations: Monthly Bulletin of Statistics, various issues; Yearbook of International Trade Statistics, various issues. **Food and Agricultural Organization of the United Nations**: Statistical Office (Rome); Trade Yearbook, various issues. **General Agreement on Tariffs and Trade**: International trade, various issues. **United Nations**: Data base.

GNP : **World Bank**: World Tables, various issues; World Tables Data base.

GDP: **International Monetary Fund**: International Financial Statistics, various issues. **World Bank**: World Tables, various issues. **United Nations**: Monthly Bulletin of Statistics, various issues. **Organisation for Economic Co-operation and Development**: Economic Surveys (Yugoslavia), 1980; Development Centre National Accounts and Statistics Department.

BALANCE OF PAYMENTS

International Monetary Fund: Balance of Payments Yearbook, various issues; International Financial Statistics, various issues. **Reserve Bank** of India Bulletin, various issues. **World Bank**: World Development Report, 1978, 1979, 1980; Country Economic Memoranda, various issues. **Organisation for Economic Co-operation and Development**: Development Centre National Accounts and Statistics Department; Economic Surveys (Yugoslavia), 1980.

OECD SALES AGENTS
DÉPOSITAIRES DES PUBLICATIONS DE L'OCDE

ARGENTINA – ARGENTINE
Carlos Hirsch S.R.L., Florida 165, 4° Piso (Galería Guemes)
1333 BUENOS AIRES, Tel. 33.1787.2391 y 30.7122

AUSTRALIA – AUSTRALIE
Australia and New Zealand Book Company Pty, Ltd.,
10 Aquatic Drive, Frenchs Forest, N.S.W. 2086
P.O. Box 459, BROOKVALE, N.S.W. 2100

AUSTRIA – AUTRICHE
OECD Publications and Information Center
4 Simrockstrasse 5300 BONN. Tel. (0228) 21.60.45
Local Agent/Agent local :
Gerold and Co., Graben 31, WIEN 1. Tel. 52.22.35

BELGIUM – BELGIQUE
LCLS
35, avenue de Stalingrad, 1000 BRUXELLES. Tel. 02.512.89.74

BRAZIL – BRÉSIL
Mestre Jou S.A., Rua Guaipa 518,
Caixa Postal 24090, 05089 SAO PAULO 10. Tel. 261.1920
Rua Senador Dantas 19 s/205-6, RIO DE JANEIRO GB.
Tel. 232.07.32

CANADA
Renouf Publishing Company Limited,
2182 St. Catherine Street West,
MONTRÉAL, Quebec H3H 1M7. Tel. (514)937.3519
522 West Hasting,
VANCOUVER, B.C. V6B 1L6. Tel. (604) 687.3320

DENMARK – DANEMARK
Munksgaard Export and Subscription Service
35, Nørre Søgade
DK 1370 KØBENHAVN K. Tel. +45.1.12.85.70

FINLAND – FINLANDE
Akateeminen Kirjakauppa
Keskuskatu 1, 00100 HELSINKI 10. Tel. 65.11.22

FRANCE
Bureau des Publications de l'OCDE,
2 rue André-Pascal, 75775 PARIS CEDEX 16. Tel. (1) 524.81.67
Principal correspondant :
13602 AIX-EN-PROVENCE : Librairie de l'Université.
Tel. 26.18.08

GERMANY – ALLEMAGNE
OECD Publications and Information Center
4 Simrockstrasse 5300 BONN Tel. (0228) 21.60.45

GREECE – GRÈCE
Librairie Kauffmann, 28 rue du Stade,
ATHÈNES 132. Tel. 322.21.60

HONG-KONG
Government Information Services,
Sales and Publications Office, Baskerville House, 2nd floor,
13 Duddell Street, Central. Tel. 5.214375

ICELAND – ISLANDE
Snaebjörn Jönsson and Co., h.f.,
Hafnarstraeti 4 and 9, P.O.B. 1131, REYKJAVIK.
Tel. 13133/14281/11936

INDIA – INDE
Oxford Book and Stationery Co. :
NEW DELHI, Scindia House. Tel. 45896
CALCUTTA, 17 Park Street. Tel. 240832

INDONESIA – INDONÉSIE
PDIN-LIPI, P.O. Box 3065/JKT., JAKARTA, Tel. 583467

IRELAND – IRLANDE
TDC Publishers – Library Suppliers
12 North Frederick Street, DUBLIN 1 Tel. 744835-749677

ITALY – ITALIE
Libreria Commissionaria Sansoni :
Via Lamarmora 45, 50121 FIRENZE. Tel. 579751
Via Bartolini 29, 20155 MILANO. Tel. 365083
Sub-depositari :
Editrice e Libreria Herder,
Piazza Montecitorio 120, 00 186 ROMA. Tel. 6794628
Libreria Hoepli, Via Hoepli 5, 20121 MILANO. Tel. 865446
Libreria Lattes, Via Garibaldi 3, 10122 TORINO. Tel. 519274
La diffusione delle edizioni OCSE è inoltre assicurata dalle migliori librerie nelle città più importanti.

JAPAN – JAPON
OECD Publications and Information Center,
Landic Akasaka Bldg., 2-3-4 Akasaka,
Minato-ku, TOKYO 107 Tel. 586.2016

KOREA – CORÉE
Pan Korea Book Corporation,
P.O. Box n° 101 Kwangwhamun, SÉOUL. Tel. 72.7369

LEBANON – LIBAN
Documenta Scientifica/Redico,
Edison Building, Bliss Street, P.O. Box 5641, BEIRUT.
Tel. 354429 – 344425

MALAYSIA – MALAISIE
and/et **SINGAPORE - SINGAPOUR**
University of Malaysia Co-operative Bookshop Ltd.
P.O. Box 1127, Jalan Pantai Baru
KUALA LUMPUR. Tel. 51425, 54058, 54361

THE NETHERLANDS – PAYS-BAS
Staatsuitgeverij
Verzendboekhandel Chr. Plantijnnstraat
S-GRAVENAGE. Tel. nr. 070.789911
Voor bestellingen: Tel. 070.789208

NEW ZEALAND – NOUVELLE-ZÉLANDE
Publications Section,
Government Printing Office,
WELLINGTON: Walter Street. Tel. 847.679
Mulgrave Street, Private Bag. Tel. 737.320
World Trade Building, Cubacade, Cuba Street. Tel. 849.572
AUCKLAND: Hannaford Burton Building,
Rutland Street, Private Bag. Tel. 32.919
CHRISTCHURCH: 159 Hereford Street, Private Bag. Tel. 797.142
HAMILTON: Alexandra Street, P.O. Box 857. Tel. 80.103
DUNEDIN: T & G Building, Princes Street, P.O. Box 1104.
Tel. 778.294

NORWAY – NORVÈGE
J.G. TANUM A/S Karl Johansgate 43
P.O. Box 1177 Sentrum OSLO 1. Tel. (02) 80.12.60

PAKISTAN
Mirza Book Agency, 65 Shahrah Quaid-E-Azam, LAHORE 3.
Tel. 66839

PHILIPPINES
National Book Store, Inc.
Library Services Division, P.O. Box 1934, MANILA.
Tel. Nos. 49.43.06 to 09, 40.53.45, 49.45.12

PORTUGAL
Livraria Portugal, Rua do Carmo 70-74,
1117 LISBOA CODEX. Tel. 360582/3

SPAIN – ESPAGNE
Mundi-Prensa Libros, S.A.
Castello 37, Apartado 1223, MADRID-1. Tel. 275.46.55
Libreria Bastinos, Pelayo 52, BARCELONA 1. Tel. 222.06.00

SWEDEN – SUÈDE
AB CE Fritzes Kungl Hovbokhandel,
Box 16 356, S 103 27 STH, Regeringsgatan 12,
DS STOCKHOLM. Tel. 08/23.89.00

SWITZERLAND – SUISSE
OECD Publications and Information Center
4 Simrockstrasse 5300 BONN. Tel. (0228) 21.60.45
Local Agents/Agents locaux
Librairie Payot, 6 rue Grenus, 1211 GENÈVE 11. Tel. 022.31.89.50
Freihofer A.G., Weinbergstr. 109, CH-8006 ZÜRICH.
Tel. 01.3634282

TAIWAN – FORMOSE
National Book Company,
84-5 Sing Sung South Rd, Sec. 3, TAIPEI 107. Tel. 321.0698

THAILAND – THAILANDE
Suksit Siam Co., Ltd., 1715 Rama IV Rd,
Samyan, BANGKOK 5. Tel. 2511630

UNITED KINGDOM – ROYAUME-UNI
H.M. Stationery Office, P.O.B. 569,
LONDON SE1 9NH. Tel. 01.928.6977, Ext. 410 or
49 High Holborn, LONDON WC1V 6 HB (personal callers)
Branches at: EDINBURGH, BIRMINGHAM, BRISTOL,
MANCHESTER, CARDIFF, BELFAST.

UNITED STATES OF AMERICA – ÉTATS-UNIS
OECD Publications and Information Center, Suite 1207,
1750 Pennsylvania Ave., N.W. WASHINGTON D.C.20006.
Tel. (202) 724.1857

VENEZUELA
Libreria del Este, Avda. F. Miranda 52, Edificio Galipan,
CARACAS 106. Tel. 32.23.01/33.26.04/33.24.73

YUGOSLAVIA – YOUGOSLAVIE
Jugoslovenska Knjiga, Terazije 27, P.O.B. 36, BEOGRAD.
Tel. 621.992

Les commandes provenant de pays où l'OCDE n'a pas encore désigné de dépositaire peuvent être adressées à :
OCDE, Bureau des Publications, 2, rue André-Pascal, 75775 PARIS CEDEX 16.

Orders and inquiries from countries where sales agents have not yet been appointed may be sent to:
OECD, Publications Office, 2 rue André-Pascal, 75775 PARIS CEDEX 16.

OECD PUBLICATIONS, 2, rue André-Pascal, 75775 PARIS CEDEX 16 - No. 42003 1981
PRINTED IN FRANCE
1100/QN (41 81 03 1) ISBN 92-64-12244-3